# GERIATRIC FU

# GERIATRIC FU

My First Sixty-Five Years in the United States.

## Octavio I. Romano-V., Ph.D.

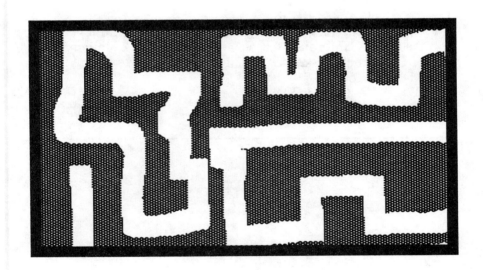

A TQS BOOK

**TQS PUBLICATIONS**
A Division of Tonatiuh-Quinto Sol International, Inc.

 PUBLICATIONS

A Division of Tonatiuh-Quinto Sol International, Inc.
POST OFFICE BOX 9275    BERKELEY, CALIFORNIA  94709

**Library of Congress  Cataloging-in-Publication  Data**

Romano-V., Octavio Ignacio, 1923-
   Geriatric fu : my first sixty five years in the United States /
Octavio I. Romano-V.
      p.      cm.
   ISBN 0-89229-018-8
   1. Romano-V., Octavio Ignacio, 1923-   . 2. College
teachers--California--Berkeley--Biography.   3. University
of California, Berkeley.   I. Title
LD750 . R66A3   1990
378. 1 ' 2 ' 092--dc20
[B]                                             89-20500
                                                    CIP

First Printing:      November, 1990

## Fu:

*A Chinese literary form which combined elements of poetry and prose. Later, it became more prose than poetry and it was used to express philosophical concerns.*

*Encyclopaedia Brittanica*

# *Dedication*

This book is dedicated to everyone who has lived to and beyond age sixty-five, no matter what country you live in.

It is also dedicated to those who have not. My heart goes out to you and your survivors. I truly wish it could have been otherwise.

And this dedication is for the 40,000 American infants who die each year before they reach one year of age, over 400,000 such infant deaths every ten years.

What if I had died before my first birthday? What if?

I also dedicate this book to all those children and adults who kept me alive physically, psychologically, and emotionally, until such time as I could do it myself. Mil gracias and many thanks to each and every one of you.

# IN THIS BOOK

**It is 1945.**

**It is 1946.**

**It is 1949.**

**It is the 1950's.**

**It is 1951.**

**It is 1956.**

**It is 1961.**

**Was it 1967? Oh, Hell, I don't remember.**

**It is 1970.**

**It is 1987.**

**It is 1987.**

**It is 1987.**

**It is 1988.**

**It is 1988.**

**It is 1988.**

**It is 1988.**

**It is 1988.**

**It is 1988.   It is 1988.**
**It is 1988.   It is 1988.**
**It is 1988.**
**It is 1989,  I am 65,  and I retire!!**

# IT IS 1923

January 1, 1923.

It is a new year.

I am seven months old, going on eight. In fifty days or so, I will be born in Mexico City.

Sixty-six years later, I will retire after teaching for twenty-six years at the University of California at Berkeley.

Now it is 1989. I decide to go to the local library and see what kind of world was waiting for me on that new year long ago. I check out the *Berkeley Daily Gazette.* Through the magic of a microfilm viewer, I rewind time. I read the date at the top of the page.

It is January 1, 1923.

I scan the 1923 headlines and articles for the first two days of that year and what follows is what I find was happening then. Wow! Does all this remind you of anything?

## WITNESS SIEZED BY
## MASKED TERRORISTS

There is trouble in Louisiana

## HILL TO FORCE LIQUOR FIGHT

House severely reprimands member who charged other
members of drunkeness.

## CUNO REVEALS PLAN
## TO END ALL WAR IN EUROPE

## NEW CLAIM MADE FOR MOSUL OIL

England and Turkey claim oil in what is now Iraq.

## PRESIDENT ASKS WARSHIP FUNDS

## TWO RESIDENCES BURGLARIZED

Thief forces back door open.

## BRITISH DESTROYER
## CAPTURES U.S. SHIP

Claim is made that ship was carrying munitions.  It is captured
off the coast of Ireland.

## BRIGHT OUTLOOK FOR BUSINESS

## NEW YEAR'S CASUALTY LIST
## HEAVY IN EAST

Revelers attack prohibition agents with chairs, tables, knives.
There are many auto accidents.

## ENROLLMENT OF ALIENS

Claim is made that alien children should be in school.
There are 7,000,000 aliens in the United States.  Education
should help in their assimilation.

## EAGER TO SELL ABROAD

Merchants and manufacturers go to Washington D.C., want
government help to open foreign markets.

## THE THRIFT THAT COUNTS

Many savings claimed by government departments.

## VERY FEW PEOPLE
## WANT PICTURE OF THE KAISER

## UC PROFESSOR'S WIFE GETS DIVORCE

Wife unhappy with University of California
associate professor.

## PUBLIC AGAINST STRIKES,
## STATES LABOR SECRETARY

## FINANCING OF FARMERS A BIG PROBLEM

Farm mortgages become increasingly unsalable.

## BRIGHT OUTLOOK FOR 1923

Business looks good.

Classified:  Sanitariums for the Aged.

Classified:  California Rescue Home for girls in trouble.

## NEAR EAST WAR HAS STARTED: LONDON HEARS

## GUARD AGAINST NEW REIGN OF TERROR

The militia is sent to Louisiana.

## ACTION ON "TWO COW" ORDINANCE

Housewives claim proposed ordinance limiting ownership to only two cows is supported by big dairy business to force small dairies to go out of business.

## GIRL BARES KANSAS BANK BANDIT GANG

Gang members identified by girl in $96,000 bank robbery.

## DRY ACT GIVEN MORE STRENGTH

Federal and state authorities are given more "get tough" grounds to prosecute offenders.

## 4 HOSTAGES IN ERIN EXECUTED

## OKLAHOMA SPECIAL PEACE LAWS

To prevent race riots.

## FILMS IN RUSSIA

In Russia, American detective films
are more popular than Chaplin.

## 170 ARRESTS ON NEW YEARS

Washington DC— Prominent government officials were much
in evidence at many exclusive hotels and swagger cafes where
the new year was ushered in with pre-Volsteadean revelry.
Prohibition agents attempted no raids.

## CITY WANTS MORE MONEY.

There is a plan to increase taxes.

## CHILDREN TO FARMS

Children from New York's congested areas spend two weeks
on a farm.

## TAFT IS VICTIM

Washington DC— Ceremony in officialdom has its drawbacks. William Howard Taft, chief justice of the United
States, is one of the latest victims of too much ceremony. He
missed a pleasant chat with a couple of sailors and was forced
to eat with senators.

## ALASKA MINERAL OUTPUT
## SHOWS INCREASE

Great interest is shown in the mineral wealth of Alaska.
Petroleum is included.

## JUVENILE COURT
## WORK DESCRIBED

"The Juvenile Court of Alameda County" was the subject of a paper given by Mrs. Leonard ver Mehr at the meeting of the social service section of the College Women's Club Thursday evening.

"In this court," she stated, "the child receives thoughtful, sympathetic and intelligent consideration, he is given hope, shown that good is expected of him, and though he has done wrong he can overcome it. Each child put on parole is required to attend church or Sunday school once a week.

"The Juvenile Court is not a criminal court," she said, "but a court for the protection and guardianship of children who need its protection. It deals with the care, treatment and control of children who are dependent, neglected, delinquent or incorrigible. Through this court the state has the authority to consider and provide for the child's future welfare at the time when the child is unable to guide his own life, or when weak, ignorant parents have failed, or when perhaps criminal parents are guiding him into crime, or when orphanage and poverty or neglect have sent him adrift, a waif with no one to whom he is responsible.

Before the differentiation of delinquency from crime the offender was treated impersonally. Whether an abnormal child, a poor child, or a mischievous one committed theft it was all the same as far as the court was concerned. The law was not administered for offenders, but for offences.

But the law discovered that it must distinguish, it must treat and not punish. The honest application of the letter of the law was seen to be not only unjust, but disastrous, defeating its very purpose, especially when applied to juveniles in this impersonal sense. The children did not understand the difference between naughtiness and illegality, nor did the enforcement of the law teach them. They came as children, homeless, guardianless, and at last the law recognized that it must receive them with an understanding of the child's view point; it must bridge the chasm between the judge and state further; these two functions are united in the latest and best legal method for handling the delinquent — the juvenile court."

## OAKLAND DOCTOR IS
## HELD AS DRUG AGENT

SAN FRANCISCO— Social workers and leaders in civic enterprises of the San Francisco bay region were startled today as news of the arrest of Dr. John Scott Barker of Oakland, charged with illegal dealings in narcotics, spread.

His arrest was brought about through the use of marked bills, the trap having been set by the state board of pharmacy. At the time this trap was being prepared Barker was giving a dinner at Oakland to social workers of the bay region, to promote the fight against the drug evil.

Information said to have been furnished by a Berkeley physician is declared to have led to the arrest of Barker. The Berkeley physician reported that a patient of his, a woman of wealth and social position, had admitted to him that she paid $90 an ounce to Barker for the drug to which she was addicted. This information started state detectives on his trail.

Those were the first two days of 1923, the year when I was born. There were masked terrorists in Louisiana; England and Turkey were fighting for Iraqi oil; homes were being burglarized; drunk driving was a problem; there was a problem with aliens; subsidies for farmers were a problem; the threat of war in the mideast increased; hostages in Erin were executed; there were racial problems; Alaska's mineral wealth was eagerly sought; rehabilitation was the thrust in some juvenile courts; and there was a drug problem.

Today things are different. We have computers.

❖

# A LIFE
# IN THE DAYS OF....

## An Introduction

My name is Octavio Ignacio Romano-V. The V at the end of my name does not mean I am the fifth of anything. Nor does it stand for a fifth of tequila. Stop with the jokes, already. It stands for Vizcarra, the maiden name of my mother. Using both names is the old custom, to identify the mother as well as the father. I like that old custom, now. But, when I was a kid, I ignored it. In some ways, I was a dumb kid.

Life was given to me in Mexico City, Colonia Roma, on February 20, 1923. A month or two later, my twenty-four year old widowed mother fled from politically turbulent Mexico. On a crowded train, with virtually no money, with two young children under five years old and an infant, she traveled north, over the central mountains and through the hot 95-100+ degree northern desert (no air conditioned trains here, kids), finally to

9

settle in southern California at the home of her mother and father who had also fled Mexico. She must have wanted to leave her children in a safe place, perhaps it was instinct, because she died shortly thereafter. We were child-orphans in a new land, left to relatives who, poor as they were, could not reject three hungry mouths. After all, we were family.

Our existence was filled with the struggle for survival, back-breaking agricultural work for meager wages (fresh stringbeans stolen and hidden in underclothes to feed the children), piece-work at fish canneries (the stench of dead fish was hard to remove from the workers' clothes, especially when they held hidden chunks of tuna fish, try lemon juice), and railroad manual labor for those who could survive the pain of creosote blisters on the shoulders from lifting railroad ties all day long for pay that would not even support a family of three.

During the nights, we were restless with fear of the immigration officers who constantly threatened to arrive without notice and deport us. When we were not frightened of them, we were upset by the social workers who wanted to break up our family "for our own good."

None of the immigration officers and none of the social workers provided a bit of music, humor, poetry, a love of nature, plants in the garden (to eat, to look at, and for medicine), an uncle's hard-earned Model A automobile, a neighbor's apricot tree to climb for an apricot lunch, fresh figs from our own tree, tortillas (now available at Safeway Stores. Can you imagine?), beans, a strong desire for a formal education for us, and hope. All that came from family.

Stolen stringbeans to feed the children, chunks of tuna fish for supper on occasion, apricots, figs, tortillas, beans, bottles of milk with the cream on top, hamburger when there was sixteen cents with which to buy a pound (eight cents for half a pound was more possible), lots of mint and cinnamon tea, and always that hope. At least there was somebody trying. My mother would have been happy. She did the right thing. She had hope for her children, even though it had run out for her.

Now it was up to my aging grandmother and her surviving children, five sons and a daughter. And even though all but one of them had families of their own to support, my uncles and my aunt somehow found ways to help the orphaned children of their deceased sister.

It was 1924 in "Old Town," the other side of the tracks in National City, a small community south of San Diego, California, not far north of the border between California and Mexico.

Several times each day, and night, too, a railroad freight train rumbled by in front of our house, about fifty feet from where we slept. The noise was deafening. But, in a strange way, it was comforting. It was regular. It was a predictable event in an unpredictable life, like the bells of the church, only more often.

Behind us were endless years of political turmoil, fear, migrations (somewhere a better life), assassinations, civil wars, and hunger, always hunger.

Before us was the Great Depression, demeaning work for the adults (when it was available), whorehouses and Prohibition liquor in our neighborhood for the rich who lived elsewhere and came "slumming" in big black limousines, segregated schools for the children, "Okies" fleeing the incredibly tragic Dustbowl disaster in their Midwest homeland, some settling in our neighborhood (migrants settling among migrants, all competing for scarce jobs, agony upon agony), hunger, a lot of interest by the grown-ups about school for the children, the hope of the Roosevelt years, and World War Two.

And then, after the war, there was a college education for me. Who would have guessed? I majored in anthropology.

College was a great, unending and exciting adventure. I wanted to take every course offered. I wanted to meet just about all the students. There were so many different types, and from all over the country. There was enough to do each year to fill the time of several years: art exhibits, archaeological digs, concerts, tennis, basketball, a library with thousands of books, and field trips of all kinds. Someone even taught me how to read seventeenth century Spanish documents. There is so much that a college can do. But I couldn't do all I wanted because I had to work all through college in order to pay the rent: dish washer, pot washer, furniture mover, car washer, bookstore clerk, gardener, making pre-fab furniture, warehouseman, advertising salesman, anything I could get and I'm sure I've forgotten some of the jobs I held.   I enjoyed my different menial jobs. There was a purpose for them, a goal.

However, there was one part of college that I never liked very much.  That was the way so many social scientists talked and wrote about poor people, as if they were almost sub-human. Many still talk like that, and I still don't like it, especially when I think about how hard the people in my family, and our neighbors, worked to obtain shelter and food to keep themselves and their children alive through illness, hunger, revolutions, migrations, living among strangers, and the Great Depression which, incidentally, was not the loss of everything for us, but a continuation of the past.  Well, *"No hay mas que seguir adelante, somos trabajadores,"* as my Aunt Trine used to say.  "We have no way to go but forward, we are workers."  And forward we moved.

Now we are in the 1980's, and often it is said that the United States population is moving away from a production type of economy and toward a service economy. In a service economy, people *talking* about what other people are *doing* become more important than the doers themselves.

This is sad because it means we are losing the sense of the importance of people whose hands actually do something, like planting stringbeans, and varnishing furniture, setting tile or pruning grapevines.

It seems that part of our nation is separating itself from the other. Increasingly, the hand part of our work is found in other lands. In this sense, the United States of today is not the same as when I was a kid, when working well with the hands was something to be respected.

Recently we had our house painted. The people who did it were master craftsmen. They did a wonderful job, stripping to bare wood, and painting with such skill that the brush strokes are nearly invisible. Then we had our solid mahogany front door stripped and re-varnished. Another masterful job. Have you ever varnished a door while it was still on the hinges, and did it so well that the finish was absolutely smooth, with not a single run?

Later, we had a new furnace installed. This crew also knew what they were doing, and it was obvious that their work was the product of years of experience. They returned several times to ensure that the furnace was in proper working order.

While the painting, varnishing, and furnace installation were going on, I was busy in the back yard, planting onions, beets, jalapeño chiles, and starting corn in planter trays. It was just like the old days, people working with their hands. For each of us, it was the mind and body together.

In a land in which almost everybody is under one kind of therapy or another (or are said by the professionals that they absolutely should be), planting and harvesting your own fruit and vegetables can be the best therapy of all.  No, I shouldn't call it therapy.  Why does everything have to be so medical?  Does this say something to you about our nation today? (art therapy, dance therapy, music therapy, sex therapy, play therapy, work therapy, eating therapy, not eating therapy, drama therapy, therapy this and therapy that). We have become a therapy society. Cripes, growing your own fruits and vegetables is not therapy, *it is living*, it is being alive, it is bringing mind and body together, just like house painting, refinishing mahogany, and installing furnaces.

Try it, y'all.

Ask the old folks.

¡Salud!

*It is 1928.*

*I am five years old.*

*I own a toy racing car, cast iron, painted a very bright red. The hood opens, revealing a motor painted silver.*

*In our back yard, at the end of a string, endlessly I pull it along behind me, making sounds like a racing car motor.*

*I dream that the racing car is real. Somehow, I am grown-up in my day-dreams, and I win race after race after race. No one can beat me.*

*Accidentally, the left hood of the toy car breaks off, but to me it is still perfect. I continue to race. Then a wheel breaks off. No matter. I will race despite everything. I am brave and daring.*

*Then, one day, my red racing car is gone. I ask and no one knows what happened to it.*

*I cry a lot over my loss, mostly at night, in bed, when it is dark.*

# ABOUT TORTILLAS,
# BOOKS,
# AND OLGA

Everybody seems to be on a nostalgia kick nowadays. Some people are nostalgic for the Sixties, others for the Fifties, the Forties, Thirties, and even the Twenties. But I have never met anyone who is nostalgic for the Tens. Actually, I believe that people have always been nostalgic about certain things and people in their past. The big difference is that today people can purchase much of the past, things like furniture, music, clothes, food, and even architecture. And everybody can see movies made in the past, in black and white, before color, thanks to television.

Sometimes I, too, think of the past, about the early Thirties. I think of a small colony of railroad, agriculture, and fish cannery workers. Some are immigrants from Mexico, but other families have lived in California for a hundred years or more. It is 1932. Near where we live, through a dirt alley and around the corner, a woman and her hus-

band have set up their small business. They
make tortillas.  They are innovative because
they use a hand-cranked tortilla machine.
Some people complain.  After all, everybody
knows that hand-made tortillas are best.
Still, the business thrives as only a small
business can among the poor.  Little by little,
and bit by bit, the man and woman are soon
selling twelve dozen tortillas daily. There is
much hunger and little work.

I am growing up, school, busboy in a restaurant, work in a warehouse, the military
draft in 1941, basic training in Wyoming,
then England, France, college on the G.I.
Bill, the University of New Mexico by way of
a California community college, and the years
are passing.  The year is now 1962 and I return for a visit home.

Even now, after many such trips, I still
cannot accept a freeway where once we
played touch football and softball, where I
would stop to play and forget to cut grass for
the chickens. Although industry has invaded
where once we played tag and cowboys, in
my mind I still see the small wood-frame
homes of so many of the people I knew.  I
return and walk through the alley which is
still there, and around the corner.  They are
still there!  The tortilla couple. They raised a
family there.  I remember them. They remember me. And they are still making tortillas. They look old even though, when I was a
young kid in the Thirties, they looked old
when I first met them.

In this nostalgia time of the Eighties,
again I think about that hard-working couple.

By selling tortillas and a few grocery items in a ten-by-ten space that used to be their living room, they raised a family of three girls and one boy. It was a good family. The last I heard of them was in 1967, when they had been in business for thirty-five years.

I count. Let's see, now, twelve dozen tortillas daily is 144. No wonder they got up so early each day. They worked six days each week. Now I multiply 144 times 6, and I come up with 864 tortillas each week. This comes to 44,928 per year, not counting the ones they made for themselves. From that point it is easy to figure that in their thirty-five years in business they had made more than 1,572,480 tortillas.

In a new way, I begin to appreciate why people get nostalgic about their past. It is not, like so many believe, that it is only a way to recreate the past or to deny the present. I think that nostalgia is a very human way of feeling and expressing a deep-felt appreciation for the accomplishments of so many people who have been a part of our lives. In my case, most of us took the tortilla couple for granted, and we would complain when they ran out of a supply. But now, looking back, wow! One million five! I like this nostalgia. It helps me appreciate people.

In my thoughts, I move from the tortilla couple to a local librarian at the public library. She's been at it for a long time. It is now today, not yesterday. Every time I have requested her help she not only provided it, but added more information which revealed a great reservoir of knowledge and expertise.

I do a lot of research, what with my degrees and all, and this librarian has always made me feel intelligent.

I think of the many librarians I have known in California, Arizona, New Mexico, Texas, Oklahoma, and back to California. Here I go again. This local librarian has worked at the reference desk for thirty-two years. I think conservatively. She has helped four people per hour, totaling at least thirty-two each day. Oh, I know she's done much more than that, but I have no way of knowing how much more. But in one week she has helped someone over 160 times, 8,320 times in one year. When she retires, she will have helped people between 250,000 and 300,000 times, probably much more. We also tend to take librarians for granted. But 300,000! Wow, again. And I have not even counted the people she has assisted by telephone.

The last time I was at the library there were three people before me. One wanted assistance about the stock market. The second requested help about auto mechanics, and the third was looking for newspaper articles about health problems during the 1960's. I was looking for historical data about state government. She helped us all and went on to help those behind me.

I like this nostalgia about today. Sure, why can't we be nostalgic about the present, about the people around us? Try it.

One evening I got nostalgic at home, about home, about Olga and our two sons, but especially about Olga. Again I begin my ritual of counting.  Good Lord!  Over 45,000 meals in eighteen years!  Dare I count the dishes and pots?  Over 628,992 times she has washed a dish or pot during these years.  Just think of the potatoes and carrots cooked, the tortillas warmed, to say nothing of the laundered socks, shirts, and pants. I need a computer and spreadsheet program to calculate what she's done in eighteen years.    And I have yet to count the hamsters, the gold fish, the chickens, the three dogs and seven pups, as well as the three cats and 16 kittens which appeared at different times during the years.

One human being has done all this, mostly for others, and this is just one house.  What about the other homes on this block?  As I drive around, now, I see houses in a different light.  I wonder how many dishes have been washed in this or that house, and I get a feeling of awe at the thought.

We live in the age of computers.  I wonder if it would be possible to calculate all the accomplishments of people like Olga. Then I think again.  I'll bet there isn't a computer big enough that could do this.  Probably never will be.

*It is  1929.*

*I am 6 years old.  We live in "Old Town,"
the other side of the tracks in National City,
California.  It is a neighborhood of poor people, mostly immigrants.*

*There is a flurry of building activity at our
house.  I don't remember much about it.  All
of a sudden we have electric lights.  There is
much talk about it, excitement, and a lot of
happiness. Just imagine, a home with electricity!  The family is proud of its achievement.  The children absorb the excitement
and happiness.  We are proud, too.*

*The next thing I remember is being told
to turn the lights off, so as not to waste electricity.*

# BILLY VINCENT

The avenue is cluttered with shops selling antiques. I see old chairs, tables, desks, and in this year of 1987 business is good. They call it a nostalgia kick. Today people pay a lot of money for furniture such as we had in 1935. We were too poor to buy anything else. Every now and then, in one of these shops, I see a particular piece of furniture that reminds me of 1935, and I remember Billy.

We were kids, just kids.

One time I took my own children back to my hometown, sort of to show them around. But freeways and industry had destroyed the material realities of childhood memories. Still, Billy Vincent's home was still there. I don't know why I didn't point it out to my kids. "There, see? That house up there atop that mound, that's where Billy lived. We were kids together." That's what I should have said, but I didn't and I still feel bad about that, not for me, not for my kids, but for Billy.

We all lived in such little houses then,
little wooden houses. As we entered our
teens, we had almost no sense of how hard
the adults worked to maintain those little
houses. All we knew was that at the end of
each day there was a bed. It was the time of
the Great Depression, a time when many of
us knew what it was to have nothing to eat,
and that common children's attire were
cardboard insoles in cheap tennis shoes with
holes on the bottom. At school my habit was
to keep my feet flat on the floor so no one
would notice the holes. Sometimes I would
forget. Surely someone noticed. At these
times I felt a deep sense of shame, and of
feeling alone in a classroom full of children.

Sometimes Billy Vincent and I would walk
home from school together. It was more
than a mile, so we had a lot of time to talk.
He was full of adventure and curiosity, excited at being alive. His father was a big, burly
Irishman, a construction worker with cal-
lous-hardened hands and a prematurely bent
back from very hard work. Billy's mother, I
believe, was East Indian. She was a small
woman, seemingly fragile, but with a pres-
ence that was felt even when she was not in
the room. She was quiet, soft-voiced, and
caring. I didn't get to know Billy's parents
very well, in that same way that most twelve-
year-olds don't ever really know adults.

Billy had his mother's big black eyes and
small bone structure, and his father's ruddy
complexion. His father had taught him to
make a crystal set, and Billy showed me. I'll
never forget the awe I felt when I first heard

a radio station on his home-made set. He even showed me how to make my own coil, and many were the evenings when I lay in bed, in the dark, listening, in that poverty-stricken neighborhood, as glamorous Hollywood night-club music came to me through the single earphone.

More than anything in the whole world, Billy Vincent wanted to fly. In that Southern California area, airplanes were everywhere, mostly navy. Billy wanted to fly one of those airplanes. It was also the days when Piper Cub planes began to make flying more accessible to the general public. Even though we were not old enough, Billy tried to talk me into taking flying lessons. By the time we were sixteen, that was about all he would talk about. It was then that I fell behind in high school, and he went on to graduate. I saw him a couple of times after that, and he had actually talked his way into getting a couple of flying lessons. Billy was still excited about being alive, about adventures that were yet to come. Now he wanted me to join the army with him because, "They'll teach us how to fly and even pay us for it. And we'll be officers!" It was 1940 and war was in the world, getting closer, especially close to kids turning eighteen.

Pearl Harbor. At the local malt shop people talked a lot, even gloated, about what they were going to do with the lands of the Japanese-Americans who were about to be removed. The military draft. Basic training in Wyoming. The soldiers-in-training constantly and loudly complained about the food.

I didn't understand.  For me, three meals a
day was a luxury.  Camp Shelby, Mississippi,
and I meet a southern belle.  Well, not exactly
a belle, but we did swing under the magnolia
tree in her front yard, just like in the movies.  New York, ugly, and then overseas to
England.  Boys and girls, soldiers and women,
hugging and kissing under tin roofs as bombs
and anti-aircraft shells burst in nearby London.  As the threat of death nears, the selectivity of love-making blurs as the urge to pro-
create and duplicate increases.  "I may not
be alive tomorrow," the GI's tell the English
women.  But, with all the German bombings,
the English women can use the same line.
Still, there were those who did not lose
their selectivity, clinging to their ideal and
the return of their "Tommies" as the bombs
came closer and closer.

The invasion of France also came closer
and closer.  It was everywhere.  Something
big was happening.  1944.  Our company was
moved to one place, then another, then back
again.  Strategic diversions, or army bungling?  We all believed bungling, of course.
Still, something was happening.  Everything
was total confusion for the GI's.  Invasion.
Cancelled invasion.  Soon. Wait. We're going.
Wait. Next week.  Wait. Pack up.  Get ready.
Be ready to leave within twenty-four hours.
Wait.

And after all our moving around, and the
thousands and thousands of American soldiers, there was Billy Vincent.  I don't know
how he located our outfit.  He had achieved
his dream.  He was flying.  He was a fighter

pilot.   P-57.   Attack fighter.   No crystal set.
A lieutenant in the Air Force.   It was an hour
or so that we talked, but talk was superficial.
His visit was all about a small box, Billy Vincent's small box for his parents should anything happen to him.   For anything, read
death.  We didn't say the word.  Not once.

France.  Normandy.  C-rations.  D-rations.
No hot food for weeks.  One day an army bak-
ing unit came by.   After days and days of
World-War II energy bars, the freshly baked
white bread tasted like cake, like a delicious
fresh-baked cake.   Even today's elite crois-
sants and San Francisco's hoity-toity sour-
dough bread do not taste as good as that
hand-torn piece of warm bread in Normandy, eaten with unwashed hands while
standing in the mud.

Tanks.   From World War I movies we had
absorbed the notion that tanks were invul-
nerable. They drive by now, and we feel the
same way.   It is an illusion, because tanks
conceal the face of human death.   In war it is
the tank that dies, not people — unless, that
is, one of your buddies is inside.

Soldiers are everywhere.  I wander about
in Northern France.  A French village.  Not a
single building remains intact, not even the
church.  A French child appears from behind
the piles of rubble. He is about the same age
as Billy and I were in 1935.   One soldier-
child offers chocolate bars and the French
child gives fresh eggs in return.   French
chickens have survived even when no building remains to house them.   The chickens
remind me of when we would wait for our

chickens to lay so we could have breakfast before going to school. I was often punished for being late, all because of those chickens, and who would believe that? "Dear teacher: Please excuse Octavio for being late to school. The chickens didn't lay their eggs until 9:30."

I am on leave in Cherbourg. I see a shoulder patch in a sea of shoulder patches. It is the same as that on Billy Vincent's jacket. His outfit must be nearby, and I am ready to go AWOL just to see my friend from childhood. The man wearing the same patch is a captain. "I want to see someone in your outfit. Where are you guys stationed.?" In my excitement I forgot to salute, or to say "sir." He didn't mind. A lot of the pilots were like that.

"We're at a temporary base near Omaha Beach. Who are you looking for?"

"Billy Vincent. He's a first lieutenant."

"I don't think you'll find him there."

"Why not?"

"I don't think he came back from a mission."

"What happened?"

"Dive bombing. I don't think he pulled out."

"Are you sure?"

"I don't think he pulled out," he repeated. Then, just like in the movies, he motioned with palm down, a dive straight down into the ground. "There was a big explosion. I don't think anyone could live after that."

"No parachute?"

"There wasn't time."

Billy Vincent died in France. He was twenty-one years old. I knew he was dead, even though the captain kept saying "I think...." He knew. We both knew.

The war is over and I am home. After traveling to so many places in the world, the little wooden houses look even smaller, even poorer. I have carried Billy's legacy to his parents for months and for thousands of miles. All he wanted was to fly. I wanted him to be home.

I knock and his mother answers. I mumble something and give her the box. I don't know what to do, but she does. With total agony and tears bursting from her eyes she screams at me, "Why wasn't it you? Why wasn't it you? Why wasn't it you?"

I didn't know why it wasn't me. "Why wasn't it you?" she screamed as the tears continued to pour from her eyes. The fragile and reticent woman had metamorphosed into a snarling tiger in pain. She wanted my death to bring back her Billy.

Several weeks later I am downtown and a man calls out to me. It is Billy Vincent's father. Shortly after receiving notice of their son's death, they had separated. "You were Billy's friend. He didn't have many friends, you know." Then he was crying. People walk by and glance at the big, burly man in overalls, then walk on. In tears and sobbing, Billy's father begs me to let him pay my way through college. "I have five-thousand dollars. Look, I can prove it." He shows me a bent bank deposit book. "It was for Billy's college education." He begs and begs, not bothering to wipe his tears. "I can work. Look at these hands. See? I can work." He holds out his hands, palms up, and they show the years of hard labor. "These hands can work. If you need money, I can work and send it to you at college. Billy can't go to college now, but you can. You can study anything you want. You can be anything you want to be."

I replied that it would be good to go to college, that I had thought about it, but I had not yet decided. I would let him know. He gave me his address. He lived in a cheap flop-house type hotel, and he carried the bank book wherever he went. "I'll let you know." I didn't have the heart to tell him I had dropped out of high school. I couldn't.

That was the last time I saw Mr. and Mrs. Vincent. I went my way. I couldn't replace Billy, either in death or in college. That was forty years ago. I was young, then. It was a time when I knew about death and fear, but I didn't know about the agony of parents when they lose a child.

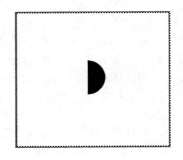

*It is 1931.*

*I am eight years old. Home from school, I must run an errand to the tiny neighborhood store for my grandmother. She tears a piece of brown paper sack and slowly writes a list for supper, about sixty cents worth.*

*Her eldest daughter is at work at the fish cannery. Work is where you get it. Her daughter's daughter, Connie, sixteen, is looking after the three Romano orphans during each day. She is a child-adult, full of a love that rubbed off on three lost kids. Such love and strength from a teenager! Connie!*

*Alex, my grandmother's youngest son, has left for work as a bartender at the local bar. Work is where you get it. He is the intellectual. A family without an intellectual is not a family. Alex is the one who gave me my first book. It was all mine to keep.*

*I watch my grandmother write slowly. As she does, I stare at the forming letters, then at the thick veins on the back of her hand. I reach out and run my fingertips along the veins. She holds still and lets me.*

*I am eight years old. What do I know?*

▶

# THE MORTUARY

"Kiss your grandmother goodbye."

The tone of voice was different. I was twelve years old and leaving for school. Whispers filled the small house. "Kiss your grandmother goodbye," I was told again. I was afraid. I didn't know why. I kissed my grandmother goodbye even though the fear made me want to pull away. She was lying in her rickety bed, my grandmother who took responsibility for us, the three orphans of her youngest daughter. Two of my uncles arrived early, before school time. That made me even more afraid. They never came that early. I knew, but I could not speak. I was sad, but I could not cry. And when my older brother and sister were also told to kiss my grandmother goodbye, I was sure, but I did not know of what. It is a terrible feeling for a child to be sure of something, but not know of what it is.

With a beans and tortilla taco in a brown

lunch bag, I walked slowly to school, my mind a sinking whirlpool of confusion. Half of me said, "Turn back. Go home. Find out." The other half accused, "You wanted to pull away!" I had never done that before. My body kept walking toward school and then from one classroom to another. I don't remember if I sang during glee club, if I sketched during art, or if I played ball during P.E. I did not eat my lunch. I wasn't hungry. Besides, I had lost it somewhere. All day I felt alone in the crowd. That was not different. I usually felt that way at school anyway.

At the end of the school day, I did not want to go home. I walked slowly, knowing all the way.

"My grandmother is dead."

Tears. My brother and my sister. Cousins, uncles, aunts. But I did not cry.

My grandmother is dead. Will the immigration officers come and take us away now? She always took care of us.

Carmen Montiel Vizcarra.

Grandmother!

I went to look at her bed, and she was gone.


All dressed up, we went to the mortuary. We took the bus. The mortuary was on the other side of the tracks. People were standing outside, talking quietly. There were so many people, family, neighbors, and some that I did not know. They were kind. They talked to every one of our family. "I am with you in your grief," they said. The words meant little to a twelve-year-old who had not cried. Still, I listened, and, as I found out later, I remembered their kind words.

I followed people into the mortuary and walked into a world I had never seen before. The silence. The whispers. But that was not all. It was the mortuary itself. It was so perfect! Wall to wall carpets covered the floor in a deep maroon, and not a speck could be seen on them. Long, white drapes hung from each window, hanging there like columns of rare marble, very still in the windless room. Even if there were a wind, the draperies probably would not move. It was that kind of room.

Everything was so neat. I have to repeat it, so perfect. The flowers were perfectly placed. The chairs were neatly arranged. The mortuary attendants were so proper. The lighting was subdued, with the major brightness focused behind the coffin which held my grandmother. The time came when I had to kiss my dead grandmother goodbye. I walked up, along the perfect wall-to-wall carpet, past the perfect draperies, down the perfectly placed chairs, up to the perfectly placed flowers, and to the coffin. I kissed my grandmother goodbye, and she was so cold. Still, I did not cry.

I did not cry until I threw a handful of soil on top of her coffin at the cemetery. Then, I could not stop no matter how hard I tried.

Ever since that day at the mortuary, I have been very uncomfortable whenever I enter

people's houses which are kept perfectly.
They remind me of the mortuary. I've been
in such houses many times since, but the
feeling remains the same. I walk in and see
perfect drapes, perfect wall-to-wall carpets,
everything in its place, everything perfectly
dusted, and somehow I get the feeling that
something is dead there, that no one is
working, making something, planting something, changing something. In such houses,
I sit on the edge of chairs, uncomfortable. I
find it difficult to talk because I want to
whisper. On such occasions, I fight against a
feeling of sadness that wants to overtake me.
And I fight against a certainty that I will
break something, soil something, spill coffee
on a divan. Did I wipe my shoes before entering? Should I leave before I do something
to destroy the perfection? Invariably, the
host or hostess seems quite at ease. Are
they worried that I might spill something?
Or are they concerned that they might do
the same?

All of this is not to say that during my
childhood our home was a mess. Quite the
opposite, everything was always in its place.
But in such a tiny house, those places were
always visible. As a consequence, I always
had the feeling that something was constantly happening, constantly changing, while at
the same time all things remained the same.
Of course, there was no wall-to-wall carpet-
ing, no still drapes which hung to the floor,
and no upholstered chairs. All that, in my
mind, belonged in a mortuary, a place of perfection, of tears and sadness, whispers,

death, and of a child who knew, but did not know what until he went there, walked up in front of everybody, and kissed his grandmother goodbye for the last time.

It is 1932.

I am nine years old.

It is nine o'clock in the evening and I am hungry.

I go to the cupboard and open it. Inside are two potatoes and one onion. That is all the food there is in the entire house where seven people live, four of them children. I look at all the other shelves. They are all bare. I climb a chair to look back in the corners of the upper shelves, to make sure there is nothing more. There isn't.

I close the cupboard.

Several minutes later, hunger drives me to look again, wanting something to be different. It is the same. I bite into one of the raw potatoes, as one would an apple. "It is not too bad," I tell myself, but I do not take a second bite.

I go to bed.

School tomorrow.

✝

# KIKO
# AND
# THE PRIEST

It's been so many years, I don't even know if I can remember all of the story about Kiko. I was a kid. It was the late Thirties. I heard parts of it during family gossip sessions. Some I picked up from my friends while playing baseball, or bean bags. Other bits I learned while hearing comments after church services, and when people said, "Stay away from Kiko. He is strange." The rest I found out while peeking, spying, and just looking around the neighborhood without seeming to be interested in anything. I was curious, like kids everywhere.

Kiko was a wino. Behind our house there was a hardware store in which, to one side, opposite the nails, bolts, and door knobs, there was a row of wine barrels with spigots, ten barrels in all. Each wino in the neighborhood had his own special concept of what a wine should be. Some liked muscatel with port. Others liked burgundy with port. There were all kinds of combinations, mostly towards the sweet. In our neighborhood, each wino was a very selective gourmet drinker. Kiko's choice was one-third port, one-third

muscatel, and one-third dry white wine. I
learned this by hanging around the coffin-
like box in the hardware store that con-
tained an illegal slot machine. Kiko would
come in and order a quart of his special
while some people played the slot machine.

Kiko regularly went to Sunday Mass. The
young, school-age boys sat up front, in the
left pews. The girls to the right. Behind
them were the parents and others who filled
the rest of the church. And in the rear, in
the last row and some standing against the
wall in the back, were the lost souls, the winos, those, that is, who would awake early
enough to attend the services and who were
not at the local bar which also opened about
the time that the church services began.

Kiko was a lost soul. Everyone said so.
Still, he would stand in the rear of the
church and look straight ahead as the priest
would rail against the damnable evils of
drinking. During these sermons, Kiko never
blinked an eye. He stood there, in the back
of the church, unshaven, black hair stubs jut-
ting from his jaw, and looking very serious,
very respectful. Kiko would cross himself
and kneel at the proper times during the
Mass, as if every word that the priest was ut-
tering was a direct message to him from
God. In my youthful years I decided that
Kiko was a good Catholic because he never
missed a Sunday service.

It must have been something the priest
said, or something inside of him, because
one day Kiko began to spend hours sitting
behind the church, on a bench at the end of

the lawn. He would sit there and think, while the neighborhood seemingly ignored his behavior. We were all used to Kiko's ways.

"Better in the church garden than in the local bar," some people said when Kiko continued his sitting sessions in the churchyard.

But one Sunday during Mass, the cleric, a roly-poly and authoritarian priest from Europe, appeared to be especially angry, which was really something because he always seemed to be very angry at us for one reason or another. He glared at the congregation. The look on his face made everyone feel as if each individual had committed some terrible sin that clearly bordered on the totally unforgivable. Sitting up front, with the rest of the boys, I tried to think of what I had done that would make the priest so angry, but I couldn't think of anything. Maybe he knew something about me that I didn't.

"Someone," he almost shouted, "is under the control of the Devil." When he said this, I wondered, who could it be? Me? I glanced at my friend sitting next to me. Maybe it was him. It never occurred to me that it might be one of the parents sitting behind us. "Someone has lost favor in the eyes of the Lord. Someone has no respect for God's house. This morning, an empty bottle was found in the yard of the church." When the priest said this, I sighed with relief. I knew he meant Kiko. Everybody knew it was Kiko.

Kiko knew it was Kiko, so did the priest. But the cleric never mentioned a name. A couple of my friends turned to look at the man standing in the back of the church, only to be met with parental frowns from the adults sitting behind us. "It is necessary to do something about this sacrilege," continued the priest. "The gates to the church yard will be locked. No one will be permitted to enter."

That afternoon, the priest was seen putting locks on the two gates. I don't think anyone cared much, because Kiko was the only person who entered the grounds, except for the neighborhood volunteer who mowed the lawn every now and then in a somewhat lackadaisical manner. A minimal offering.

By Tuesday, the neighborhood was buzzing with talk about Kiko. People had seen him in the churchyard, but he was not sitting on the bench or even drinking wine. He had brought a broom and rake with which he was gathering the dry leaves and putting them into a couple of paper sacks. The grounds were left very clean and neat. "Kiko wants to atone for his sins," people said. Some were laughing at his behavior. Yet, the locks were still on the gates. I wondered how he managed to get into the grounds in the first place.

"There will be no exceptions!" Now, during the service on the following Sunday, the priest was shouting at this affront to his authority. But a lot of people thought that Kiko had done a good thing, and they were irritated at the priest's harsh words. Still, there would be no exceptions.

Maybe it was the wine. Or, maybe Kiko did not understand. I had heard people say

that too much alcohol hurts the brain.   On
Wednesday, while returning home from
school, I saw a man mowing the lawn in the
church yard.   At first I thought it was the
regular volunteer, but when I got closer I
saw that it was Kiko. He did not have a grass-
catcher on the lawn mower, so he carefully
raked the cut grass into little piles which he
put into paper sacks.   Bouncing a worn tennis ball, and pretending I had not noticed
anything out of the ordinary, I moved toward
the gates and saw that the locks were still
there.  How did Kiko get in there?  Then,
kicking the tennis ball along as in a game, I
played around the edge of the grounds until I
stumbled onto Kiko's secret. At a corner he
had cut along the wire fence, bent it back to
enter, then straightened it to appear as if
the fence were intact.   Immediately, without
even the slightest thought otherwise, I decided to keep Kiko's secret to myself.    I
would not even tell my best friend, which I
did two days later, but only after he swore he
would tell no one else.

   "Permission!"   the   priest   thundered.
"Authorization!  No one has been given permission, nor has anyone been authorized to
work in the church yard.  Yet, it has come to
my attention that someone has taken the lib-
erty.  This has got to stop.  If there is anyone
who seeks the good graces of the Lord, then
let that person do it properly.  Let that person come to Confession, to absolve all sins.
Perhaps, then, and I say perhaps, the Lord
will consider work in the Church yard a
proper way to cleanse the soul. Until then,

absolutely no one is permitted onto the grounds." That was the closest the priest ever came to actually naming a specific person, or to making a deal with the "sinner."

A week went by, and no one saw Kiko, either at the bar or in the church yard. He was also absent from Sunday Mass. This was unusual, but people hardly commented about it. Winos, it seems, are quickly forgotten when they are not seen. During his sermon, the priest was not choking with anger. He was just normally angry with us, as he was all the time. Meanwhile, the church grounds looked better than ever.

Then, all of a sudden, the entire border of the yard had been lined with flowers; geraniums, daisies, and marigolds. I noticed it on the way to school, and I was sure the flowers had not been there the day before. "Kiko," I thought. "He must have planted them during the night." The grounds looked very pretty. "If everyone sinned like that," my cousin said that afternoon, "it sure would be a better world."

The next thing we knew, Kiko was dead. An accident in the drunk tank, somebody said. Not many people came to the simple funeral services for Kiko. Maybe it was just as well because the priest decided to speak only in Latin. Nobody ever knew what it was that he chose to say about Kiko. I understand that during eulogies you are supposed to say only good things about the departed. But, in this case, I'm not sure. None of us understood Latin. And, besides, that European priest was always mad at us.

*It is 1933.*

*I am ten years old.*

*My uncle Fred takes me hunting. There is no meat for dinner. We go hunt for quail.*

*After considerable walking through scrub-brush, he finally flushes a covey of quail. They take off with flapping wings. Quickly, he raises his shotgun and shoots twice, missing both times.*

*For some reason, the quail begin to circle and then fly straight toward us, flying within easy range. But my uncle doesn't bother to reload.*

*"Why didn't you shoot?" I ask him.*

*"I get the first two shots," he replies. "They get the third."*

*That night we had beans and tortillas for supper, no meat.*

*I was happy for the quail, but it was many years before I understood my uncle.*

# THE ALTAR

When I was a child, the altar always meant that place in front of the pews of St. Anthony's Church. The altar was a private place, a mysterious place, a place of secret powers, a place of awe and reverence, a place with a tiny gilded door atop a gilded mantle which held secrets beyond earthly imagination, a place fenced off, a place forbidden, a place that was always deep inside the insides of the church.

And because it was so inaccessible, I rejected it. It was in this manner that I was launched upon a life's journey which, when all is said and done, has been nothing more than a search for the power to open that tiny gilded door and not be a passive viewer, to be, instead, a participant, a party to the private, a knower of the mystery, in touch with the secret powers, a giver as well as a receiver of awe and reverence, and to be a part of that which is beyond earthly imagination.

Over the years, I have felt this way in the New Mexico desert, while in the northern mountains of New Mexico, the Rio Grande

Valley in south Texas, by the ocean, while fishing in a California lake, while picking up a stone, while watching a squirrel, while listening to a mocking bird, and even in my own back yard.

Recently, I planted a healthy looking bare-root, bare-branched nectarine tree in a large container and it just sat there, not doing what trees are supposed to do, which is to sprout tiny buds after a reasonable length of time, then produce bright green leaves, and grow, big and healthy.

But it wouldn't, and it wouldn't. Every day, before going to work, I would go out to the back yard and minutely inspect the half-inch trunk of the nectarine tree and the three branches it had grown before I purchased it. All was bare and remained so for what seemed like months. I would look at every spot on the little tree and, in time, became familiar with each of them. I would also look at the base of the trunk and at the tips of the branches. Nothing. I called the nursery and they said, cheerfully, "Bring it back. We'll give you a refund. Be sure to bring your receipt!"

But I couldn't.

And I didn't.

I continued with my daily inspections, sometimes twice and even three times a day.

Once I had almost given up. But then I scratched the fragile bark and underneath it there was a thin film of green. I gave it more water, even though the mixed container soil didn't appear to need it. About a week later, I scratched the bark again and it was still green.

Perhaps I had planted it too deep. I carefully dug into the soil and raised it. When I did so, I noticed that I had not mixed the soil properly, leaving in too much of the clay-filled dirt of our backyard. It had not drained properly and had become soggy. When the tree did not grow, I added more and more water. I guess I over-watered it because the roots of the little bare tree were sitting in a puddle of muddy, clay mush.

I scratched another spot on the trunk, and it was still green. "The tree lives."

After that, each morning, I took to removing about a half-inch of soil from around the edges of the container, to let it dry out, leaving a mound which held the tree in the center. This went on until I had removed some six inches of soil from the edge. Let's see now, six inches, a half-inch per day, I must have done this for twelve days or more, each time letting the top of the soil dry out a little more, but keeping the bottom moist.

During all of this time, I continued with my daily inspections. By now that poor little tree had received many scratches on its trunk and branches where I had checked for color under the bark.

Hope was dimming within me.

One morning the soil under the tree seemed especially dry, but I held off giving it too much water. Routinely, I began the careful inspection. There it was. A tiny and pointed green growth, obviously the beginnings of a leaf, about three inches above the soil, facing the sun.

Maybe. But I wanted to be sure.

The following morning there were two more leaves breaking through the bark.

"Attaboy! I knew you could do it," I said out loud, with a feeling of awe, great joy, mystery and, yes, reverence. Again I spoke to the tree. "I knew you could do it." There was a smile on my face as I touched the budding nectarine tree several times. "Yeah," I said, almost in a whisper. "Yeah. I knew you could do it."

It had taken so long. I turned and looked at the other growing plants in the yard. It was nothing I can explain, but I saw them in a different light now. I walked around, looking at each one. There was the small apple tree, a tangerine, orange and cherry. Nearby was a pineapple guava followed by bush beans, pole beans, scalloped squash, cherry tomatoes, and zucchini. The apricot tree had filled with green leaves, as had the peach and pear trees. A small patch was covered with celery plants, the result of one stalk left to go to seed the previous year. Onions, cilantro, oregano, garlic and garlic chives were growing. And there were weeds under the prickly pear cactus. Each year, the cactus provided us with delicious cactus fruit and young, tender leaves to eat. The strawberries were planted, as were the bush peas, finger carrots and corn. Petunias added color, as did the geraniums and sweet william.

Mint and spearmint plants were winning the battle against more weeds. On the other side, beets were producing leaves near jalapeño chiles, bell peppers, and Italian sweet peppers. Poinsettias were trying to turn red at the wrong time of the year. Parsley (two kinds), potatoes, an olive tree, a lemon and a lime tree, a fuschia, chard, bougainvillea, and a red rose of Castille dotted the rest of the place. No lettuce was to be seen. I've never had much luck with it. Scattered about was a wheelbarrow, shovel, hoe, rake, and trowel.

Sparrows, finches, squirrels, mourning doves, pigeons, and blue jays were consuming birdseed scattered on the ground. I saw a few snails, a slug, spiders, ants, blue-gray sow bugs, worms, and, oh, oh, dog poop near a mound of dirt in the corner of the yard. A wandering white butterfly stopped briefly on a lemon leaf, but on this day I had not seen the hummingbird. Along the wall of the garage, two grape vines were sprouting after a dormant winter.

In the midst of all this growth I felt religious, like being in a church, just as I had been long ago when I was a child. Now, in the garden among the endless shades of growing green that surrounded me, I felt that I was literally inside the insides of a church. I knew I was. I knew it for certain, because I could feel it.

The struggling nectarine tree quickly filled its branches with long, slender and pointed green leaves. In a couple of years it will produce pink blossoms and bear red-purple-colored fruit with a very sweet, soft and whitish meat inside. Now I have something more to look forward to, along with the fresh beets, peas, corn, cilantro, jalapeño chiles, cactus fruit, apricots, peaches, and all the rest, including the chard, cabbage and fresh, home-grown celery.

Some weeks later, I am watching television and I hear Bear Heart speak. Bear Heart is an American Indian medicine man. He says, and I write it down, "Every day is a holy day. Let your every step be a prayer. A blade of grass is holy."

Upon hearing Bear Heart, all the elements of the years come together.

I realize consciously what I have always known in my heart.

The inside of the inside of a church is the earth.

One day I was sweeping out the cement-covered driveway. It had cracks. There, in one of the cracks, tiny celery plants were groping toward the sun. I watered the crack, the celery grew until I cut it, and we had a delicious soup.

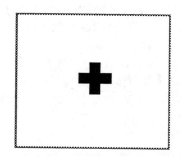

*It is 1939.*

*I am sixteen years old.*

*In high school, I am getting A's in mechanical drawing.*

*I am getting F's in everything else.*

*I drop out of high school.*

*I get a job as a pot-washer in a big restaurant. I receive a paycheck every week. I have money to spend.*

*Still, within my mind, I dream that someday I will return to school and study to become an architect— not just any architect, but a good one— so good that I become famous.*

# THE
# HEALTH WORKER

It was during the days when tuberculosis sanitariums were commonplace, and the law said that people diagnosed as having the disease had to be taken to one for treatment. If anyone refused, the law also said that they should be picked up and forced to go. Sometimes individuals did not take kindly to being locked up in a medical facility, and they attempted to escape. But, in most cases, security was tight. That's the way they did things during the Fifties, and New Mexico was no different.

Armando Abeyta, on the surface, was no different, either. He was a health worker. Specifically, he was an investigator for the tuberculosis control program. His job was to locate people who had been identified as having TB and to attempt to convince them that they should go to a sanitarium voluntarily. He was good at it, believed in his work, and for those reasons the medical people depended upon his talents more than they did the other investigators. After all, he had a Masters Degree in health sciences from the

University of California at Los Angeles, and
he was bilingual in Spanish and English. This
enabled him to work effectively in both languages, a desirable ability in New Mexico's
health services.   In college, he had a minor
in literature, especially poetry, and by family
tradition Armando was an accomplished san-
tero, a wood-carver of religious figures, an
Hispanic art which has made New Mexico
world famous. Accordingly, Armando Abeyta
moved in many circles, the scientific, the
poetic, and the traditional Hispanic.   And
who is to say that the three are so different?
People can be scientists, poets, and traditional all at the same time.   Nowadays, so
many people have the habit of moving only in
their own circle, usually that which is determined by their own particular profession.
But there are also those who move in circles
not determined by profession, but by personal preference and an attitude towards life.   In
such groups, you can find artists, plumbers,
professors, and santeros. It was in such a situation, a mish-mash of people who got together in Santa Fe, New Mexico for a party,
where I first met Armando, and this is the
story that he told me.

*I got a call.   It was from my supervisor
and it sounded urgent.   A man had escaped
from the tuberculosis detention center in
southern New Mexico.   My assignment was
to track him down and to get him back to
the sanitarium, no matter what.   After all,
the man was a threat to the general public.
His name was Anastacio Gallegos, and since*

the Gallegos family was well known in northern New Mexico, I felt that my job was fairly
easy.  All I had to do was go around and ask a
few questions and, presto, I got my man.

And that is exactly what happened.  I'm
good at my job, after all I am a trained professional. Within three days I had a lead and I
reported it to my supervisor who said, "Get
him back."

The information I had took me first to a
home in the outskirts of Santa Fe, and from
there to the village of Gallina in the mountains of northern New Mexico.  I had to visit
two or three homes there before I got a hint
that his mother lived north of there, high in
the mountains and a distance from the main
two-lane highway leading toward Colorado.
"About a half-hour from here, turn off where
you see a pile of stones by the side of the
road.   Then continue to the end of the side
road.  That is where his mother lives."

I drove north along the highway and, sure
enough, I saw the pile of stones.  I turned off
and drove along an unpaved road, rough,
with ruts.  Obviously the road had not been
taken care of for many years.  There was
little need, apparently, for there were no
ranches or homes along the way.  I drove and
drove, slowly, worried about the oil pan of
the car and the rocks in the road.  It was fall,
trees were turning yellow and red, and the
day was chilly.  I must have driven fifteen or
twenty miles and was beginning to think that
I had been given false information when I
saw smoke in the distance.  That must be
where the mother of Anastacio lived.

As I continued on my way, I began to prepare what I was going to say, and to say it politely. If he was there, I was reasonably sure
I could somehow talk him into returning for
treatment. After all, I had built up a pretty
good record in such cases.

Nearing the isolated ranch on the top of a
hill and surrounded by meadows, I spotted
someone by the side of the house, cutting
wood for the winter. There was an enormous pile nearby. He was a young boy, about
seventeen. When I asked if this was the
home of Anastacio Gallegos it was immediately clear that the youngster was mentally
retarded. "Mother," he said, "Mother," as he
pointed toward the house. I knew that anyone in the house was aware that I had arrived, but no one came out as one might expect. I knocked on the door and it was
opened by an old woman who, surely, must
have been at least eighty years old. She
spoke in a small voice and said "Yes," when I
asked if this was the home of Señor Gallegos.
I explained my mission and she invited me
into their home.

Mr. Gallegos was about fifty years old, and
he was cutting venison, preparing to dry the
meat for the coming winter. We sat and
talked for about an hour.

The old woman was his mother, and she
was the third generation of her family who
had lived at the ranch. She was eighty-two.
The mentally retarded boy was his oldest
son. His wife had gone to California with the
other children. Winter was coming, and
while during the spring and summer months

*the woman and boy could manage with a little help from relatives, the cold months ahead were another story. They had to prepare for deep snows and very cold weather. Yes, the boy had chopped all that wood, and in the late spring he planted vegetables. He also cared for a dog and two goats. Without him, the mother could not get along, and the opposite was true because the boy could not have survived alone at that isolated spot. Winter was nearing and there were repairs to be made. The roof leaked, a couple of cracks in the walls needed patching. Food had to be put up for the winter. Someone had to hunt for meat. The three needed each other to prepare for the coming cold. The house had only two rooms. He showed me the other and it was full to the brim with supplies for the winter. They lived in the other room during the cold months. It was kitchen, bedroom and living room.*

*As carefully as I could, I explained my mission and Mr. Gallegos did not disagree with any part of it. He knew he was sick because hunting had become harder and harder. Against all my training, I accepted a cup of coffee. We talked of the mountains surrounding the ranch. It was talk of love and hardship and many generations. Finally, Anastacio Gallegos suggested that I permit him to remain there for the winter, to see that the boy and the old woman were taken care of, and if I would agree to that he would wait for me to come back the following spring. He would return to the sanitarium for treatment, he said. But my instructions*

*were to bring him back. "I am not allowed to
do that," I told him, "I could lose my job."
My voice was weak, for we were both thinking the same thing: who would take care of
the woman and the boy? He sensed my hesi-
tation and said no more, leaving me with my
thoughts, my conscience, and my profession,
all swirling within my head.*

*"The best I can do," I finally replied, "is to
make the recommendation to my superiors.
They will have to make the decision."*

*It was getting late, and I wanted to get
back to the highway before dark. Señor Gallegos, his mother and the boy walked me to
the car. The stillness of the mountains surrounding us was broken by what seemed to
be a very loud motor, my car's intrusion into
the moment of our thoughts for the future.
They stood there, smiling their farewell. "We
don't have many visitors," the woman said. I
turned to her son and said, "I am not without
influence, Mr. Gallegos." He must have seen
something in my eyes because his reply was,
"Thank you. God go with you."*

*The return to the highway was just as ar-
duous as the arrival, and it was dark when I
drove toward Santa Fe. It was Friday. I would
not have to report until Monday. Nevertheless, on Saturday morning I went to the office. The building was empty except for a
couple of janitors. Pulling out a* REPORT OF
FIELD TRIP *form, I rolled it into my typewriter.* TIME IN, TIME OUT,  MILEAGE. *I filled in
the necessary details and stopped when I got
to* PROJECT AND RECOMMENDATIONS.

*Looking out the window, the Sangre de*

*Cristo Mountains were capped with large*
*New Mexico clouds, whiter than white*
*against the blue sky. I don't know how long*
*I sat there, thinking of nothing and every-*
*thing. Finally, my hands moved to the keys*
*of the typewriter.*

Re: Anastacio Gallegos

Tuberculosis Case Number: A-616538B.

Purpose: Return to sanitarium for treatment.

Pursued search from Santa Fe to
Gallina. Despite every possible effort,
patient was not found. Winter snows
are approaching. Will resume search
in the spring.

*It is Spring of 1942.*

*Betty and I are on a date. She is Irish, blonde. I am Chicano. We met at work at a warehouse. We talk a lot about the war, and should we get married. We are on a bus in San Diego, on our way to a movie. The bus, like the city, is full of sailors.*

*All of a sudden Betty says, "Let's get off at the next stop." I am surprised. We are still many blocks from our destination. She insists.*

*When we are off the bus I ask, "Why get off here?"*

*"Didn't you hear those sailors behind us?"*

*"No. Why?"*

*"They were talking about killing that Spic with the blonde. They meant you."*

*Two months later, I was drafted to go fight fascism overseas. In England I read about the sailors of the United States Navy who repeatedly attacked Mexican Americans in Los Angeles.*

# EDUCATION

It was many years ago, about as far south in Texas as you can get, right on the edge of the Rio Grande River. I had gone there from California to do fieldwork for my degree in anthropology. At first, one of my professors did not want me to go. It was to be a study of a small community comprised of people of Mexican ancestry, and the professor said that I could not be objective because I was born in Mexico. I would be too involved, he said, and I would not be scientific. To this I replied that if it were true that one could not study one's own people, then virtually all sociologists in the United States, as well as all historians of American history, should be dismissed immediately. He said that was different. I went to Texas anyway.

That was when I met Don José. He was a very respected elder in a small cluster of homes inhabited by very poor agricultural workers. The neighbors had granted him the title of Don because he always behaved in a respectful manner, treating everyone with

respect and equality.  He even treated powerful and wealthy people as equals.

Don José owned a small, two-room house
that was vacant.  He had built it next to his
own for his older son who did not need it
because he had obtained work as a janitor at
a school which provided living quarters.
Since I wanted to live in the community, I
approached him about renting his house. We
sat and chatted, getting acquainted, learning
about each other.  After all, perhaps I would
not want to rent from him, or he might not
want to rent to me. In the course of our conversation we agreed on the rental, and the
talk turned to the topic of money. "How
much can you pay?" he asked.  I had come
from northern California where rents were
very high. After an exchange of more information, I finally offered my absolute rock-
bottom, fully expecting to pay more.  Well,
we could always haggle. "I can pay sixty dollars a month," I said. Don José was silent for
what seemed a very long time. Finally, he
said, "I don't know what the rents are where
you come from, and you are a stranger who
has not learned about this area. For now, why
don't you offer thirty dollars per month?"

That was how I met Don José.

As a field research method, I had selected
"participant observation."  It means that you
participate in the community's activities
while observing for research.  It sounded
good in the classroom, but picking cotton in
ninety-eight degree humid Texas heat was
something else. The long canvas bag that
trailed behind me was so heavy it felt full

even before I began to pick. At the end of four hours of picking the cotton, I took the bag for weighing. I had earned all of forty-five cents! Don José, with a smile, said, "Don't forget to send some of that home." I laughed, but later I thought, "What if I were doing this for a living?" I looked out across the field. It was teeming with men, women, and children. All but the extremely young were working.

One evening I took Don José across the border to visit his relatives. On the way back we stopped to buy a bottle of tequila. I selected a bottle priced at twelve pesos, and, this being Mexico, I decided to haggle over the price. "There must be some mistake," I told the young girl behind the counter, feigning mild shock. "I can buy this same bottle for less at another store." The girl replied, "One moment, Sir, I'll ask my father about the price." She disappeared behind a curtain and I could hear their voices. I was getting ready to pay ten pesos when she returned and said, "Yes, Sir, there was a mistake in the price. It is fourteen pesos, not twelve. My father apologizes for the mistake." I paid the fourteen, knowing that I had been had by the father of the girl. And all through this episode, the serious expression on Don José's face did not change a bit. He neither laughed at me, nor did he scowl at the owner of the store. Like I said, Don José treated everyone with respect and equality.

As Don José learned more about the nature of my anthropological fieldwork, he invited me to meet a friend of his who lived in a nearby town. "I think this would be of some importance for your work," he had advised.

It was raining the afternoon we drove toward his friend's house, along an unpaved street, skidding on the mud, past house after house where more poor people lived, where there were no sidewalks, where glimmers of hope sprung from the soil in flower pots and gardens. It was the television of the day, watching plants grow and bloom.

"Here," pointed Don José. It looked like the other houses. Unpainted, because fifty-cents an hour, when there was work, did not provide for the luxury. The weathered wood on the outside wall had turned dark from the wet of the rain. The fence, with many missing slats, no longer served its purpose. Untamed grass had overpowered struggling domestic plants, leaving only red geraniums to fight it out to the end, which they were doing.

Yes, there was the anticipated screen door, torn, hardly protecting the inner door of faded pine. And, yes, the hinges squeaked, still resisting the encroaching rust, a losing battle, a matter of time.

Inside, it was difficult to carry on a conversation, especially one of importance for anthropology. The noise of the constantly dripping rain through leaks in the roof into several metal buckets and tin cans impeded the progress of science.

I turned to look at the large poster on the wall, at which I had only glanced upon entering. It was a large replica of **The Universal Declaration of Human Rights.** Nothing in my entire university training had prepared me for this experience. The poor, I had been told over and over again, were interested only in grubbing for a living, leaving no time and no inclination for more lofty or even abstract ideas.

On the way home, Don José and I talked little. I was anxious to return so I could write my field notes before memory failed. But memory did fail. I could not recall most of the words spoken by Don José's friend. All I could remember was the replica of the Declaration, there in a poor man's home in south Texas, where buckets and cans caught the water from the many leaks in the roof.

I recalled an outdoor barbecue, sponsored by the settlement's mutual aid society. It was held under the mesquite trees in a nearby field where a small chapel had been built many years before. The barbecue had been prepared in the old way, wrapped in several layers of wet cloth and placed in a hole in the ground, in the ashes and stones heated by a large bonfire the night before, and then covered with dirt. There were tortillas, beer, and goat meat so delicious it would have made the chefs of fine restaurants envious.

When everyone had had their fill, Don José addressed the small group. Standing on the steps of the chapel, he spoke of history and the ideas which had influenced its course. In his discourse he mentioned Pablo Neruda, Gabriela Mistral, the philosophy of Benito Juarez, Octavio Paz, and others. He also spoke of Abraham Lincoln, Henry James,

Rousseau, Voltaire, and Franklin Delano Roosevelt. I can still hear the soft voice and the words of Don José, there under the mesquite trees' meager shade that hardly shielded us from the hot sun. And it was there, although I did not become conscious of it until much later, that I began to question that very strange traditional custom of the social sciences to never consider the poor as capable of intellectual and abstract thought, much less having such thoughts appreciated by a group of people who picked cotton for a living, and who traveled to Michigan in trucks to work in sugar beet fields.

"They call him Joe," Don José's older son had said to me one day. "Who do they call Joe?" I asked. "My father. The growers in Michigan call him Joe. They do that in Oklahoma, too." But at home in his own community in Texas, he was always Don José.

And it was Don José who told me one afternoon, as we sat on his front porch, "In these days everyone who goes to school is said to be 'educated.' But I don't believe that people are 'educated' in schools. What they get in school is instruction I think education comes only when you learn to use your instruction in a way that helps people, and does not do them harm."

I think that Don José, who had achieved the thirty-second degree as a Mason, was a very educated man, even though he didn't get past the third grade in grammar school.

*It is November, 1945 and World War II is over.*

*After three years overseas, I return. We land in New York.*

*I get a pass and walk a street, any street. I stop at the first malt shop I encounter. I enter and order a big, thick chocolate malt.*

*For months and months and months and months I have dreamed of this moment.*

*Enjoy.*

*The place is full of soldiers. Apparently they had the same dream.*

*The soldier sitting next to me turns, and, with an ice-cream mustache on his upper lip, he says, "Worth fighting for, huh?" There is a look of sheer happiness on his face.*

*"Yeah," I reply. I don't know about my face, but I sure have a deep feeling of sheer happiness inside.*

*Tomorrow I leave for California, and home.*

# A STORY
# FOR CHRISTMAS

I am in my car, driving home from work. I live in a California city where many families live. I always hope that people will drive carefully in my neighborhood. There are many children here. A child may forget and step into the street. That is very dangerous. Sometimes a car comes down our street, moving very fast. If I am in the front yard, I yell at them to slow down. I worry about our own two children. I worry also about the other children in the neighborhood.

Some of the children laugh at me when I yell at the cars that go too fast by our house. Maybe they think I am crazy. But, that is all right. I prefer to see them laughing at me than to be hurt by a speeding car.

One night I was returning home a little late. I stopped to buy presents. Then I waited to have them all wrapped with pretty paper. Christmas was nearing.

The freeway was full of cars, and they were moving so slow that I took another road home. I was driving by some houses when I saw something I had not seen in a long time: *luminarias,* brown paper lunch bags with about an inch of sand on the bottom. A candle was put in the sand. There were about a hundred bags that had been placed in rows around the front yard of this house. A candle was burning in each one. It was beautiful.

It reminded me of New Mexico. I lived there for a while, and during the Christmas season the Hispanic people would line their yards and homes with *luminarias.* The soft candle light shining through the paper was prettier than any electric lights. The candles were meant to light the way for the Three Wise Men. They took the place of the star.

People still light luminarias in New Mexico. But I was surprised to see some in California. I stopped my car and went to the house to tell the people who lived there that I enjoyed what they had done. I rang the doorbell. A man came to the door. He was about sixty-five years old, and he told me that he was from New Mexico. His wife was also from there, from a village in the mountains.

He invited me in for some chocolate. He and his wife were alone. Their children had grown up and left. Two were married and had their own families. One was a doctor in San Francisco, and the other was a policeman in San Diego. Their daughter was in college in Oregon. She wanted to be an architect.

The man told me all about the children

they had raised in California. He and his wife remembered all the things the children had done, the times they were sick, and their adventures in school. And they remembered when each one left home.

"It used to be very noisy around this house," the woman said. The man nodded to agree with his wife. Every time they remembered something about their children, they smiled. They were very proud parents.

"Every year I put out the *luminarias*," the man said. "But it is not to light the way for the Three Wise Men. I put them up to light the way for our children, so they won't forget us for Christmas."

I looked out the window and some people had stopped in front of the house to admire the pretty light of the candles. A couple of cars driving by slowed down as the passengers looked at this New Mexico sight in California.

"Oh, yes," the man said. "The luminarias have become a Christmas feature in this neighborhood. Many neighbors come to see them. They know we light the way for our children. I have told them a million times." He laughed. "I probably bore my neighbors because I tell them the same story every year, but they listen politely."

"Are your children coming this year?" I asked. Then I was sorry, because a look of sadness came over the faces of the man and woman.

"This year they will not be home for Christmas. They have things they have to do. But they write and call us on the telephone.

We are very happy when they do this."

"Perhaps," I said, "both of you can come to our house for a Christmas dinner."

"You are very kind," was the answer, but they wanted to be home, just in case.

"We will be very lonely," the mother said.

"Yes," her husband added. "We will be lonely, and we will be happy, too. Our children. One is a doctor, one is a policeman, and the third will be the best architect in the country. We will be lonely and happy at the same time."

"And we light the way," she added, "just in case our children come home for Christmas."

I returned home and looked at our children. They were happy with the presents I had brought. There was happy noise in our house. And there was the wonderful smell of a pot roast cooking.

After they had gone to bed, I sat alone in the living room. I tried, but I could not imagine our home with the children gone. I know they will grow up. Will their mother and I be lonely when they are gone? Yes, we will be very lonely. Maybe we will also be happy at the same time, like that couple I met tonight.

*It is 1946.*

*It is two o'clock in the afternoon and I am still in bed.*

*In the next room, my aunt and her daughter are talking, keeping their voices down to almost a whisper. Still, because of the thin walls, I can hear the sounds if not the words.*

*I am convinced that their lowered voices are a sign of respect for me as a returned veteran of World War II. I take a moment to appreciate that. Even though I had been home for many months, I still remember how happy they were to see me return safely, and how worried they had been.*

*I am curious. What are they talking about for so long? I get up and tiptoe to listen at the crack in the door.*

*They are wondering why I don't get off my butt, get a job, and go to work.*

# THE PHOENIX
# WITHIN US

## An Introduction to a Book

Have you ever started to write a book and, after many months, completed only the introduction? Well, this is such a case. My book is about illness and adversity, and there certainly are many books about this subject. But this book is more. It is about that particular element or elements of human character which bring together both mind and body during illness. Humans, as I'm sure we have all noticed, do this in such a way as to make it possible to learn from experience. If we didn't do this, most of us would not be here today. Very often, therefore, people convert an encounter with illness and adversity into a positive contribution toward personal growth.

"What?" you may ask, "illness and adversity are positive forces?"

"They can be," I will reply, "even though we know that this idea is contrary to much that we have been taught in school, and almost all that we hear around us every day."

That's because we are citizens of a nation that produces highly specialized experts on practically every single adverse experience we can possibly have or imagine. We have experts on the social, psychological, and the physical, each of which is chopped into smaller and smaller bits and specialties. As a consequence, we ourselves tend to become subdivided agglomerates of bits and pieces. In this context, we have lost the sense of ourselves as unified wholes who can, as such, participate in the total process of life as integrated and total organisms.

But total human beings are endowed with self-healing and regenerative powers. And as natural organisms, we are capable of growth due to adversity, we learn from it, and we use that newly acquired knowledge of self in the future course of our own personal lives. Quite naturally, we try to pass this on to others.

However, despite all our specialists and experts, detailed, and even not detailed, knowledge of this particularly outstanding and holistic human characteristic, the ability to learn and grow positively following an affliction, is strikingly absent in the professional literature that deals with health and illness. This neglect has created a major gap in what we know about what happens to people after a debilitating experience, and how we incorporate it into our everyday lives in ways that quite often change its quality, often visibly improving it.

Illness and adversity, of course, is the stuff of which novels and poetry are made. That

is well-known. What is not known is the role
that these experiences play in the normal
course of human events; how we learn from
them, and how they may change our lives.
What also is not known is the relationship
between debilitating personal conditions and
how people who have suffered them have
gone on to great achievements.

For example, thirty years of severe abdom-
inal pain was the experience of Albert Ein-
stein, yet it did not noticeably hinder his
monumental work. What was the relationship between his pain and his work? A similar affliction plagued Sigmund Freud. And,
during the last forty years of his life, Charles
Darwin was beset with serious attacks of nau-
sea, shivering, and faintness. He needed
constant rest during this time, being able to
work only a few hours each day. It is interesting that it was during this time that Darwin wrote his greatest works.

The list goes on. Socrates had epilepsy.
So did Dostoevski, while Flaubert suffered
from chronic depression. Thomas De Quin-
cey was addicted to opium. Proust was an
extreme hypochondriac, and Stephen Haw-
king, the brilliant British physicist, is afflicted with amyotrophic lateral sclerosis. Many
others can be added to this list, among them
Charles Dickens, H.G. Wells, the outstanding
sociologist Max Weber, Vincent Van Gogh,
Berlioz, Mary Baker Eddy, Robert Louis Ste-
venson, Helen Keller, and Franklin Delano
Roosevelt.

The achievements of these people are
well-known. The relationship between their

accomplishments and their afflictions, however, is not. Yet, I cannot help but wonder,
did their personal conditions somehow con-
tribute to their achievements? And what is
the relationship between suffering and
achievement? And why is it that some people manage to surmount it, even use it, while
others do not?

Illness and adversity, then, can be causes
of personal behavior change. They can also
be related to social and cultural change. Specifically, major personal changes can result
from having someone close to us undergo a
serious or even fatal accident, as witness the
impact that Candy Lightner's experience has
had on our society as a result of the death of
her child by an intoxicated driver. She went
on to form MADD, Mothers Against Drunk
Driving. The thrust of her entire life
changed following the experience. A similar
example is that of Norman Cousins who was
afflicted with cancer. His life was changed
as a consequence, and he went from editor
of a literary magazine to university professor
of health.

As for the rest of us who are not so famous, don't we all seem to know someone
who went on to become a doctor or an accomplished nurse as a result of a serious illness? Others who undergo an affliction have
had their lives changed in a different way,
and they go on to become patients' advocates
with an intent to improve health care.

There are many such people who have
found a purpose after an illness. Many such
people later become active participants in

the American Red Cross, the American Cancer Society, the American Heart Association, as well as many other such organizations. In these and other similar cases, separated analytical variables and isolated statistics cannot possibly capture the personal intensity which such experiences can have on human life, nor can they capture the profound meaning that adversity and illness can have for individuals.

From all that I have said, it should not be assumed that affliction and subsequent or concurrent productive behavior is principally the domain of famous people. The Phoenix within us is much more widespread than that. After talking to many people about this subject, it became clear that almost everyone had something to say about learning from illness, and about personal changes in behavior and values as a result. There was a case in which survival from an airplane crash led a father and daughter to "rediscover" each other, and to find a new meaning in life. Similarly, the death of her husband led one woman to "rediscover" her long dead parents and their example of how to overcome adversity, a lesson which she now passes on to her own children. In another case, a personal triumph over alcoholism led a man to a career in public health and the desire to help others. There are many more examples, such as that of a man who suffered a serious skull injury and subsequently "learned" how important his wife and children were to him. One young man I talked with suffered a gang-related stabbing. The experience turned his life away from destructive behavior and toward constructive activities. And an American Indian friend lost his father to cancer. Hurt and subsequently lost, he became self-destructive until later when he discovered that he, too, had cancer. The last I heard of my friend, he was in remission and had forsaken his destructive behavior in order to help poor people in Texas. For still another friend, a mastectomy was a very serious problem. But during her experience she discovered the love that so many people had for her, and of which she had not been aware. That knowledge, learned while she was in the hospital, has sustained her ever since, and she applies it to everyone around her, everyday.

When we think about it, the title of this book, *The Phoenix Within Us,* is really a statement of faith in people. In another sense, it is a statement of our everyday reality, about the world in which we live, about the people we know, and about the resiliency and the self-learning courage of so many human beings. In still another sense, "The Phoenix Within Us" is a statement of the history of humanity.

It is sad, I believe, that all too often we have assumed that the afflicted have been useless burdens. In some very extreme cases, this may be true. But it is also true that the sick and the wounded, rather than being useless, can also be our teachers.

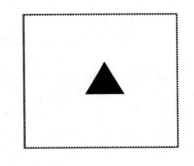

*It is August, 1949.*

*I am driving across the southwestern desert, returning to the university in New Mexico after working during the summer in California. I am driving a 1934 Plymouth, fifteen years old, with chugging motor and worn tires. Then, flat tire, left front, out in the middle of nowhere, with no spare and just about enough money to reach Albuquerque. It is three in the morning,.*

*A trucker, in a semi, stops. "I'll send help from the next town," he says after learning of my predicament, and he takes off in a roar.*

*I wait. I wait for more than an hour.*

*In the distance, a truck is coming toward me. It is the trucker who was going to send help. "Here," he says, as he unloads a tire. He had to wake a friend to get it.*

*He helps me put it on, and we pump it up with a hand-pump. As we work, we talk. He about his life as a trucker, I about my life as a student.*

*For his help, I offer a third of my money, ten dollars. He refuses to take more than two. His gasoline, going and coming, cost more than that.*

# PABLO'S STORY

Pablo had put in about twenty or thirty years work in bureaucracies, federal and state. It was hard to tell exactly how many years because he would never say. But in talking with him you knew it had been a very long time. He told me that he had hoped for a change of assignment here, a promotion there, something more interesting or even meaningful. The promotions he got, but the rest was not forthcoming. He found little personal fulfillment in the work he had done for so long. So he quit. He was a head honcho in a bureaucracy one day, and out of it the next. "I quit," he had said one day, and he did. He was a little over fifty years old.

After his self-induced change Pablo wandered about, but not irresponsibly. He began to get re-acquainted with his community. He decided he wanted to help, and he did. He helped save a community clinic for Hispanics so it could continue to serve the poor. He helped a small publishing company because he believed strongly in the value of reading and providing literature for the Chicano community as well as for all who were interested in this field of endeavor. It should be said that he helped many individuals who came to him with their problems because Pablo was that kind of person. Still, there was that restlessness, an emptiness, the lack of fulfillment he had felt for years. That was when he and his wife decided to return to Mexico, the land of his parents. They left one day, their destination a cluster of small farms outside tourist-filled Puerto Vallarta. They had distant relatives there. Over a year later, they returned. That was when Pablo told me this story. And when he told it, I knew that in it he found a little of what he had been looking for all of these years.

*About two kilometers from the ranch where we were visiting, there lived an old man. We got to know each other quite well. We spent hours just talking, and I learned that his family had owned their small tract of land for over two-hundred years, weathering cycles of political and social turmoil. He grew vegetables on his land, and in one segment he had planted about twenty square yards with string beans. He was a good farmer, and he knew how to care for the soil. In that region he was known for the fine vegetables he produced.*

*The string beans were about two feet tall when caterpillars invaded and began to eat away at the plants. It wasn't long before they had spread to almost the whole field, and it became clear the old man would not have* string beans to sell at the market if something was not done.

The next day I borrowed a pickup truck and went to town to buy some insecticide in order to help save the man's crop. When I returned, I told him what I had done. It was all new to him, for he had never used an insecticide before. Carefully I explained about the off-white powder, what it would do, how to apply it, to be careful, and to wash well after using it.

After that, I was busy with other things for several days, and I did not return to the man's plot of land. When I did, I immediately noticed the powder had been spread on all the plants except for one small corner of the bean field. When the old man came out to greet me, I asked if he had run out of insecticide. No, in fact there was a sufficient quantity left over. Then I suggested that perhaps the small section in the far corner might need some more. I didn't want to offend him by suggesting he had not done it properly. "No, it doesn't need more," he replied. "I didn't use it there." When the old man saw the question in my face he explained. "Well, we are all God's creatures; you, the people around here, the animals and the trees, even the string beans. The caterpillars are God's creatures, too. If I leave that corner for them, I will have my string beans to sell at the market, and the caterpillars will have a place to live."

*It is a 1950's winter in Albuquerque. I am a senior at the University of New Mexico.*

*I live in a small, fifteen-foot canvas trailer. Outside, it is nearing twenty degrees. Snow and ice cover the ground. Inside, I wear two pairs of winter underwear, two pairs of trousers, two heavy shirts, a wool sweater, and a thick Army overcoat.*

*I am studying for an examination the next day, and it is hard to write while wearing two pairs of gloves. The small burners on the cooking stove do not help much.*

*The next day I take the exam, and my grade is a "D."*

*Oh, well, win a few, lose a lot.*

# THE THREE DREAMS

**Dream One**

Last night I had a dream. Or did I dream it during the day, when I was thinking? I dreamed that another world war had begun, and the people who could stop the killing did not exist. It was a matter of a few weeks before the entire world was consumed by vast atomic explosions and subsequent fires which made ashes of the green of the forests, charred to death cats and chickens, raccoons and squirrels, made ashes of the corn in the fields and converted the river waters into deadly poison. Not even the mottled quail remained to walk the earth, and the winds were the music of a wake.

Then, suddenly, from the direction of the setting sun, a great white crane, a male, swooped down from the sky and glided gracefully over the black stumps which had been trees. The crane flew toward a marshy lagoon, left there by the changing flow of a river. As the bird spread its wings to land, a dark red gash was exposed on its side. The last living creature on earth had been badly wounded and partially blinded by some explosion. Weak and staggering now, the great white crane drank water from the murky lagoon. As he turned away, he came upon the inert body of what remained of a female crane, once also white, now gray from the ashes upon which she had fallen and then struggled to get up.

The male looked at the body on the ground. Then, though seriously wounded and half blind, he turned to face the silent heap of feathers and began the slow rhythmic movements of an imperative and majestic dance. Half in the air, half on the scorched ground, the male gracefully danced a half circle around the female and returned to his starting point. Three times he repeated the half circle. And, although no reply came from the limp body, he continued his dance. Now he spread his wide wings and leaped lightly into the air, floating back to earth seemingly in slow motion. Again he danced around the female. The movements of the dance agitated the chest wound, and it began to bleed. The crane hardly seemed to notice. Soon, the remaining light of the day was passing. Still the great white crane danced all around. Once he leaped into the air and flew a short distance, as if to leave. But he returned to his dance. Twice, in the twilight, he fell. Twice, slowly, he raised himself to dance again, resuming his ancient patterned movements. There, in the final receding glow of the sunset, the man-made wound finally vanquished the white crane. He struggled to stand again, but he could not. The bird had fallen in the ashes of what once had been large and still growing trees.  His final act was to turn his head and look once more at the dead body of the female.  It was while doing this that the last living creature on earth died.

**Dream Two**

My second dream was a time-warp through fifteen summers in a row, all at once, and each summer was like the others. "Do you want some tomatoes?  Ours are falling to the ground." "Need some lemons?  We just can't use them all." "We have lots of cabbage. Want some?"

It was our neighbors talking to each other, and it had been like this for years and years. I am dreaming about people's yearly urge to plant, cultivate, and grow their own food even in this urban residential area.  In almost every yard, during growing season, there are more fruits and vegetables than people can use, so they offer them to each other.  But, as it happens so often, too many people have planted tomatoes, or squash, and there is  no one who wants more.  So they spoil, like the lemons.  In our block alone there are about ten lemon trees in back yards, producing so many lemons that they just fall to the ground and spoil.  And at the local stores, each lemon costs twenty-five cents.  The same happens with apple trees, grapefruit, and peaches. But in my dream, all of this changed.

An elderly man with a truck that seemed
equally old began to drive around the neighborhood, leaving notice at each door that on
Saturdays he would return to collect the excess fruits and vegetables from people's
yards. Everyone took to the idea, and that
first Saturday he drove off with boxes and
cartons of cherries, apples, oranges, peaches, lemons, limes, chard, spinach, onions,
squash, tomatoes, and more. People took to
the idea because he was on his way to deliver
the produce to elderly people, to outlets for
the poor, and to programs for the homeless.

Now all this back-yard produce would not
go to waste. The old man and his truck
made the people feel good about themselves.
The entire effort was like a good war. And
who would have imagined that so much produce was grown in the back yards of a city?
The word spread. There was a story in the
newspaper, followed by reports on radio and
television, right there with the other news
about violence, fires, drugs, accidents, and
death. Then came the news that people in
other surrounding cities were beginning
similar efforts.

Then it all ended.

Government officials had learned that people in the neighborhood had been giving
small amounts of money to help the old man
support his truck. The representatives of
the state determined that such money was
"income" and, therefore, taxable. The produce man was duly informed he must ac-
quire a business license, or form a non-profit
corporation with a board of directors and

corporate officers.   In addition, he would have to pay taxes for disability and unemployment insurance.   He would be required to purchase insurance sufficient to cover all possible contingencies.   "It's for your own protection," the state people had informed him, "in case someone sues you."

Then they gave him samples of the quarterly financial reports he would have to complete, including one for the newly raised tax for mass transit.

With all this facing the old man, he sold his truck in order to pay a claim for back taxes; city, state, and federal.   And that's the last the neighborhood saw of him, except for one evening during a brief television interview.   "Well," said the old man into the microphone, "there's not much a person on Social Security can do.   All I wanted was to be useful."

**Dream Three**

This was a very busy dream.   So much happened.   And, again, I don't remember if I dreamed it while asleep or awake.   There was exciting news.   The radio, television, and newspapers were all reporting the same story, repeating it over and over. Nuclear war had been banned, and the dismantling of atomic weapons was proceeding rapidly.

"The white cranes live!" I shout silently to myself. Then the dream quickly changes to the old man and his truck.   I am that man! I am confronting one bureaucrat after another, making them retreat like pitiful wimps. Having accomplished this, I return to the neighborhood and resume the collection of homegrown produce for those in need. It is late summer, and there is much to haul. Once again the people give me money to support my truck. I refuse anything more. "No, thank you," I say modestly, "All I need is a little money for gasoline." Then I am driving toward the poverty center for the elderly. I am whistling a tune called *Adelita.* I had learned it long ago, when I was a child in a place far away from here. It is a song of struggle, regeneration, and hope.

*It was 1951.*

*To continue my studies at the University of New Mexico, I applied for a John Hay Whitney Opportunity Fellowship for Minorities. I really did not expect to receive it, but I did.*

*A big part of me couldn't believe it. Why would anyone in New York give me money? Why would they want to help me?*

*The experience set off a train of thought in my mind. I began to think of all the people over the years who had helped me in one way or another. There were so many that I began to make a list. The list got longer and longer.*

*I did not complete the list. I quit at 152! The experience was humbling.*

*All I could think was that there sure were a lot of people who had been there, and tugged up on my bootstraps, when I needed them.*

*When I graduated, they were not present at the ceremonies, but they were with me.*

*They are with me now.*

# OF TIME, SPACE
## AND THE PEOPLE OF
## THE UNITED STATES

Many years ago, during the late Forties, I hopped into my 1934 Plymouth and traveled to Mexico City. While there I went to visit my godfather whom I hadn't seen since childhood. We talked of many things and he told me much about the history of Mexico. He played a phonograph record of Aztec music. As I listened, it seemed to me that the native Mexican music was very similar to the music of the Navajo Indians of Arizona. As a token of my visit, I wanted to purchase a record of Navajo music as a gift for my godfather, so I asked him where I might find it. He insisted that in all of Mexico City such a record could not be found. I was disappointed, since I had become used to finding such items easily in the United States. As I left, I promised to send him the record.

The years passed and, ultimately, I found myself teaching graduate students at a large university. Periodically, I would become irritated with the students because of what seemed like their incessant complaining.

Well, let's be honest. A lot of it was just plain whining. Did I do that when I was a graduate student? Yes. Still, I continued to be periodically irritated. These students had so much going for them, including swimming pools, a bowling alley, restaurants, a theatre, concerts, lectures by internationally known persons, art galleries, visiting dance troupes, and so much more, all on the campus.

The Sixties had passed, leaving a legacy of the problems faced by the people of the nation, while other problems were emerging as focuses of national concern. And, it seemed, people all around me had nothing to talk about except to utter a continual litany of "what's wrong!" What struck me, however, was the fact that so many of the students' complaints had little or nothing to do with the major problems of the nation. Instead, the negative litany had to do with the little things in everyday life. I took to standing around in the halls, or sitting on the lawn, listening to conversations. Almost invariably, the discussion I listened to focused on something that was wrong, from the elevators in the building to complaints about the weather, lunch, a movie, a class, whatever. So much dissatisfaction.

One weekend, away from all the complaining, I decided to copy my small collection of records onto tape. It was forty or fifty records in all, collected over a span of some thirty-five years. There was a record of El Trío Los Panchos, and one of El Trío Calaveras. Of course there was one of Pedro Infante. People who know these records will really date me. And there were a couple of records of good Mariachi music, which always seems to be in style. Then I browsed through the other records: Respighi by Philharmonica Hungarica; Yugoslav folk songs; Flamenco; Strauss waltzes by the London Philharmonic; George Córdoba playing the music of France, Portugal, China, Algiers, Mexico, Philippines, Spain, Brazil, Colombia, Greece and Italy; The Nonsuch Explorer with music of the Far East, India, Africa, the Americas and Continental Europe; the incomparable Segovia; the trumpet of Rafael Méndez; Bachianas Brasileiras No. 5 by Heitor Villa-Lobos; Stravinsky, Bizet, Ravel; the Virtuosi di Roma playing the music of Albinoni, Vivaldi, Pergolesi; Pablo Casals playing Schumann; Manuel de Falla's "Three Cornered Hat" played by a Swiss symphony; Debussy; Tchaikovski's "Violin Concerto"; Bach's Suites for Cello as played by Pablo Casals; Dvorak, Chopin, Brahms, Liszt, Mendelssohn, Handel, Boccherini, Beethoven, Gounod; the guitar of Laurindo Almeida; Calypso Christmas with the De Paur Chorus; Bela Bartok; and Carlos Chávez conducting the National Symphony of Mexico; koto music of Japan; Navajo chants; Eskimo music; and music of the Andes.

Then it hit me. The world of music through time and space, was at my fingertips. My collection was small, but it could have been so much bigger had I chosen to purchase more. And, I could have, what with sales, close-outs, and special bargains, to say nothing of regular prices which, for records, have never been that much. Can you imagine? Segovia for $5.95? Ancient Greek music for $4.50? Traditional Japanese Koto for $5.45? Quite a few of these records were purchased when I was on a meager budget as a college student. What a marvel in this small collection! Quickly, in my mind, I flashed back to the stores where I had bought most of these records. They were small stores, several of them mom and pop type businesses. My mind also pictured the many, many record catalogues I had seen in the record stores. What an incredible range! The music of the ages, from every corner of the world and back as far as written and remembered music has existed, all available in the stores or on special order. Tibetan prayers, Gregorian chants, Egyptian songs, Russian, Argentine, Medieval, Renaissance, Hawaiian, Apache, Mongolian, Irish, religious music, harvest songs, music of birth, music of death, music of celebration and joy, all were available in recorded music along with whatever musical fad was in style at the time.

And almost all of it was made possible through the facilities of those two often maligned enterprises, technology and business. It is a miraculous achievement which exists under our very noses. Never in the entire history of all humanity has any nation, or any people, made available practically the entire musical expression of the world, both in time going back to the dawn of history and in space spanning the entire globe.

I thought of my godfather in Mexico City, with a limited range of music available in the record stores. And I thought of the complaining students who seemed unconscious of this miracle of technology, business, and human expression which was all around them. Nowhere else in the world has this happened, I wanted to tell them. And, when all is said and done, perhaps it is fitting that it should have happened in a country such as the United States in which the people's roots are almost as broad and far ranging as the music which they have recorded and made available to everyone.

I confess that as I was thinking these thoughts I was somewhat overwhelmed by an urge to go out and grab people, shake them, and shout, "Look, look! Look what has been accomplished in the United States! See? Everything is not negative!" I tried it a couple of times, with somewhat dismal results. Maybe I didn't shake hard enough.

As so often happens, one thought led to another. There it is! There, in my living room. Books. No, not just these few books. Lots of books. Published materials. Printed materials. That's it. Libraries. Within the walls of our major libraries, from New York to California, there exists what I believe to be the most extensive collection of written and printed expression ever collected in the entire history of humanity. Maps, books, manuscripts, letters, magazines, journals, newspapers, newsletters, specialized collections, English, foreign languages, documents written by immigrants, documents written by Native Americans, art, poetry, history, government documents, millions and millions of items, and, like the music on records and tapes, the library collections represent history's most extensive collection of human expression in both time and space. What is equally spectacular is the fact that our libraries and their contents are available to anybody and everybody on a daily basis. No other nation has made this possible, ever.

Unbelievable. Absolutely unbelievable.

My memory mind, in a mini-microsecond, flies back to a day in the early Thirties. My uncle offhandedly gives me a book about electricity. I can still see it, feel it. I would open it often, glance at the contents, not understand a bit of it, but it was my book, my reservoir of knowledge, my door to the world beyond the walls of our house, an unknown world, but an exciting world nevertheless, full of promise, yes, full of promise, full of adventure, and fulfillment, all in a little black book about electricity. It was like wanting to fly.

No. I did not become an electrician, or a specialist in electronics. But, even to this day, I still love that book my uncle gave me as if it were a real, living thing.

Then, my mind, quicker than a computer, travels back to Texas during the Fifties, when I was doing anthropological field work in a small community of Mexican American migrant agricultural workers. One evening I am visiting a family, getting some information. A question about history comes up in the conversation and no one knows the answer outright. "One moment," the father says, "perhaps the answer is here." He crosses the room and picks up a book. It is a book on world history. A big, heavy-set man who had labored hard all of his life, he holds it in his calloused hands and thumbs through the pages. This moment is immediately fixed in my mind, and I recall it as if it were happening this very moment. It was not the question. Nor was it the answer that impressed me so much. It was the absolute gentleness with which he handled the volume, conveying a feeling of awe, great value, and respect.

Then my mind races across space and time again, this time to the library at the University of New Mexico, and I am being taught to read seventeenth century manuscripts written by the Spaniards who settled in the area. The handwriting on the documents are works of art done by master scribes. Such patience. Such dedication. Later, I am reproducing murals painted by Pueblo Indians in the twelfth century, to be published and housed in the library. The murals are a precious legacy, found fifteen feet below the surface of the New Mexican desert.

Still later, for the first time, I found myself in the stacks of the main library at the University of California at Berkeley. I walked around in utter disbelief. Room after room, floor after floor, shelf after countless shelf, thousands upon thousands of books, journals, and magazines, all within easy reach. I pulled down volumes at random and, before I knew it, five hours had passed. It was like walking through Pueblo Bonito at Chaco Canyon, the great Mayan temple of Chichen Itza, the Taj Majal, and Stonehenge, all at once.

As I left the library I looked at the caretakers of this monument, the librarians, and
I saw them in a new light. They served the
needs of over twenty-thousand students and
faculty here. I thought of the many libraries I
had visited, and the hundreds of questions I
had asked of their caretakers. I thought of
the guidance they had given me, and I came
to truly believe that most librarians are highly competent research associates without the
title.

Recently, I visited the main library in Oakland, California. As I walked from department to department, I saw people from just
about every walk of life: very young children,
teenage students, business men and women,
poor people, the elderly, others dressed in
obviously very expensive clothes, Blacks, Hispanics, Asians, Pilipinos, and Anglos all busily reaping the fruits of a dream of long ago.

At the Oakland Library I was looking for
newspaper reports dated about ten to fifteen
years ago. And there before me was the type
of librarian whom I'm sure we have all met at
one time or another. He was a veteran,
clearly having worked many years in his profession. I told him what subject matter I was
looking for, and he not only guided me to
the main sources, he kept bringing more
published materials as I reviewed the first
articles. By the time he was through, I not
only had more than enough of what I needed, his new sources and knowledgeable comments about them opened and guided several new and fruitful avenues of research. But
that was not all. He handled each article,

each page, each newspaper that he brought to me with the same reverent gentleness and respect as that migrant farm worker-father in Texas who leafed through his book on world history as if he were handling the Cullinan, the world's largest and most valuable diamond.

I think about these people, librarians and citizen users of libraries, and then I think of politicians. When the going gets a tiny bit tough, one of the first things the politicians cut is community library services. Of course they protect their salaries, junkets, their per diems, their gas mileage, their health benefits, their dental benefits, their psychiatric care benefits, their legal benefits, their generous vacations, and their discretionary funds. In their self-serving thrust into the taxpayers' pocketbook, on any pretext whatsoever, the politicians are more than willing to cut this incredibly valuable lifeline of the American psyche and sincerely genuine American culture.

Tragically, in my opinion, the California public school system has followed the example of the politicians, or vice versa, for it has relegated its public school libraries to the virtual bottom of its spending priorities. I hope that this is not happening in other states, because if it is we are all in a heap of big trouble.

But in spite of these setbacks to our cultural storehouse, the incredible continues to happen in some libraries— computers.

It used to take weeks, often months, and sometimes even years of delving into card catalogues or leafing through volumes of abstracts in order to develop a basic bibliography for research. Now, for many subjects, an enormous step in this direction can be accomplished within a matter of minutes, and you have a bibliography printout.

In the health field, for example, entries covering over 4,000 journals and numerous specific subjects are readily available on computer. And for general library holdings, the University of California lists 8,810,800 publications and 1,178,472 periodical holdings in nine different libraries! Time and space have become more readily available to the everyday users of library services.

Computers, however, have not made the personal services of librarians obsolete. Quite the opposite. Over and over, while standing around library desks or library computer terminals, I have seen librarians still giving personal attention to library users, giving hints, directing people to research sources, introducing them to a new book, and doing all the other things that librarians have always done.

While it is true that the holdings of American libraries now represent an achievement which is absolutely unique in the entire history of humanity, and while it is similarly true that the dedication of librarians has been of such great value that it will always be without measure (we will owe them forever, while we have paid them so little), it is equally true that the bedrock of this entire accomplishment has been the dreams and visions of people long ago, in a partnership with the continuing support of the American taxpayers.

Yet, when politicians don't get all the money they demand, about the first thing they cut is our libraries. This certainly tells us something about the caliber of our elected officials.

We live in the days of airplane hijackings and the taking of hostages.

Should we allow our politicians to hijack and hold our libraries hostage, and threaten to kill them, unless we give them all the money they demand?

*It is 1956.*

*I am thirty-three years old.*

*I am doing anthropological field work in south Texas.*

*Lucas, about twenty-seven years old, and I are sitting on the front steps of his father's house.*

*Across the street, Juan is polishing his new black Mercury. It is new to him. Actually the car is many years old, with dents in the body, and a motor that lets out a lot of smoke.*

*Juan finishes his task, and takes off in his car.*

*Lucas turns to me and says, "Have you noticed? Every time Juan takes off in his car he jerks his head back so people will think it has a lot of pickup."*

*I laugh. It reminds me of the one about the man who drives around in ninety-eight degree heat with the car windows rolled up so people will think he has air-conditioning.*

# THE WASHING
# OF THE BIRDS

The San Francisco Oil Spill of 1971

It was the eyes of the birds, not the beaks or the oil-encrusted feathers or the feet or tails, but the eyes of the seagulls, the scoters, the loons, mallards and grebes that held my attention, compelling from my soul an apology to the soul of each bird whose eyes, in turn, somehow became mine and through which *now I see the many people milling about, the many boxes and tubs of mineral oil, rags, cornmeal and flour, as hands behind me bring still more rags and more mineral oil to clean the black guck from my blackened feathers* and Chico, my seven-year-old son who went with me to save the birds, says, "What do we do now, Father?"

*I tried to fly, but the heavy oil on my wings and the human hands would not let me.*

Neither my son nor I knew at this time that only a few of the afflicted birds, perhaps ten percent, would survive even after a thorough bath of mineral oil. We learned that later. People of all ages had come to help save the birds. Now they hovered around and talked quietly or laughed nervously among the birds that flapped and squawked and screeched, their cries filling every inch of available space in that enormous warehouse in Richmond.

Now word spreads rapidly that people are needed at the beaches above San Francisco. We rush off to help there. On the way the car radio is tuned to the news and from a helicopter an announcer says, "I hate to say it at a time like this, but the oil makes the water look like a big, beautiful rainbow."

We arrive at a long stretch of beach north of San Francisco. The sands at water's edge are covered with ugly globs of oil, tar, and hay. The hay had been strewn there to catch and hold the oil. There is only one person in sight, a young boy, perhaps fifteen, with no tools, lifting handfuls of hay and sludge and moving them, handful by handful, away from the water's edge. Beyond him is more than a full mile of black-edged beach. It is at this water's edge that my son says again, "What do we do now, Father?" I look up and the lone boy is returning to the water's edge for another handful of oil-sand-hay.

All of a sudden we hear the sound of heavy motors as tractors and trucks arrive to clean the beach. Each vehicle has a small crew. My son's voice, launched on a journey all its own, floats toward me above the noise of the surf and diesel engines. "The tractors and trucks are cleaning the pollution on the

sand, but their motors are polluting the air,"
and I say, "That's a good joke, son," and he
says, "I'm not joking, Father."

Through the day, and the night, and the
next day, people are washing the birds that
had been trapped by the filmy rainbow from
the Golden Gate.

Back at the cleaning center, someone has
thrown clean, fresh Q-tips, cotton, and gauze
among the oil soaked rags to be carted away.
We pick them up and return them to where
the fresh supplies are kept. "Three-hundred
more birds are coming," everyone murmurs
at once. Next to me, a middle-aged woman is
tearing strips of paper for the bottom of the
cages in which more birds will be placed. "I
never get the glamour jobs," she says, and we
smile like we had known each other forever.

A girl of thirteen or fourteen sits for more
than a half-hour with a loon, slowly and very
gently caressing it. "I'm trying to calm it
down," she says.

I think to myself, "For the young people
here, the structure of existence is gone, and
it is gone for the birds, too." But, perhaps a
new existence has been found, that of saving
life.

We help load a garbage truck with hundreds of heavy pounds of rags soaked with
mineral oil turned black from contact with
countless birds' feathers. Our hands and
clothes become blackened, like the birds
themselves.

The next morning, at the bay's edge by the
racetrack, the birds are clean. The oil spill
has not reached them. Two people dash up

and seem very angry because there is nothing to save there. Even the motor of their Volkswagen sounds angry as they drive off, away from this water's edge where the birds are still clean and flying.

It is ten at night, where rocks protrude to be tapped and lapped by the wavelets of the bay. A male voice. "Some ecology people told me to come here and move the hay to the road where it can be carted off. But how in hell can anyone work on those rocks in the dark?" The man is around forty-five, accompanied by a daughter in her teens. As he speaks she stands there quietly. Then the man blurts out, "Those goddamned oil companies! Something has got to be done about them!" I think the man wants to communicate with his daughter. But there is so little that can be done that he stands at the water's edge and curses the dark.

Back at the ecology center, rows of cages are lining the cement floor, rags cover each cage to calm the birds. It is like a morgue with sheets covering the bodies, except that every now and then one of the bodies will screech or quack or squawk. Ten percent or less will survive, even after being cleaned. Two thousand five hundred have been processed.

Another day has passed and the newspaper headlines proclaim: WINNING THE BAY CLEANUP FIGHT. What a strange and tribal process which changes the washing of dying birds into a victory. Sacrifice or requiem?

It is a sacrificial ritual. What else can you name it when the death of 2,250 birds and countless other forms of life is called a victory? After all, when birds are dying, isn't it better that they die clean?

It is almost over. So many people went to help. At night, my son Chico is sitting in the living room, drawing pictures with crayons. In the style of a seven-year-old, he draws a flying bird. "What kind of bird is that?" I ask.

"It's a Giant Heesha Bird," he replies as he continues to draw on a large piece of paper. Later I look again. He has drawn some airplanes, and the bird is bigger than any of them. The bird dwarfs everything on the page. Finally, down below the bird, way down below, he draws blue water and a tiny oil tanker.

Anyone looking at that drawing could tell right away that the Giant Heesha Bird, if it chose to do so, easily could forever destroy that tanker with a single peck of its beak.

*It is 1961.*

*I am visiting a family in New Mexico.*

*They own a nursing home which is located next to their house. Nursing care is given to about twenty elderly patients.*

*That evening, an aide comes to the door and informs the owners that, "Mrs. Gutierrez has died." She was eighty-four years old.*

*I learn that Mrs. Gutierrez had no known survivors, so there is no one to notify. What had she been like when she was young?*

*The thought of her dying there, so alone, overwhelms me, and all of a sudden I feel I have to do something.*

*I get my guitar and go out to the yard. I turn and walk to the center of a large, empty field nearby. There, alone, in the dark, I raise the guitar and sing Mrs. Gutierrez a Mexican love song, La Malagueña. "What beautiful eyes you have..." the song begins.*

*When I get to the third line of the song my eyes become flooded with tears for this unknown woman. As I continue to sing, the tears flow down my cheeks and drip on the guitar.*

*All of a sudden I am aware that I am smiling. I am singing, crying, and smiling all at the same time. "For you, Señora Gutierrez," I whisper in the dark. "Para ti...."*

*When I finish the song, I have the feeling that I have done something really important.*

# THE DINER

Restaurants.  Seventy-eight restaurants all located within an urban area of six large square blocks.  I know.  I work in this California city, and I counted them.  I walked the area with a notebook, taking note of each one.  The restaurants try to crowd each other out in a particularly American pluralistic food struggle for business survival.  Almost daily I drive or walk by several restaurants. New ones open, others close.  Each new establishment opens with a flurry of hope, crowded with local bureaucrats, office workers and students.  Will customers return?

Each lunch hour I leave my office in search of ...what?  There is an urge.  Perhaps a croissant stuffed with chicken in herbs.  Or, perhaps a pork burrito with jalapeño chilis. Mandarin beef?  Patterson's custom sandwich, with tender ham?  There seems to be no end to the choices.  I can even have a hot dog, while a couple of health food stores sell a myriad of sandwiches all of which taste like alfalfa sprouts no matter what else they may contain.  Or, how about a Polish, or frozen yogurt? Italian fried chicken? Pizza. Lots of pizza. Japanese tofu? Not only Japanese food, but also Vietnamese, Korean, and Thai.

Every time I walk these streets, I seem to pass by Joe's Diner. It is an old, old place in an old, old building, with a long counter with over twenty ancient stools. Joe's Diner is interesting to me because during all hours of the day people are sitting at the counter. I don't remember ever seeing it empty, like some other restaurants in the area. I wonder why people are always eating there. Must be good. There must be something about that place. Maybe it is one of those hidden jewels, an unpretentious place that pays little attention to appearances and focuses on good food. That surely must be why someone is always eating at Joe's. It must be a place like those truck stops one hears so much about, plain but excellent food.

Once I stopped at the window and looked at the menu. It sounded solid enough, nothing really fancy, breakfast, lunch, sandwiches, and a soup of the day, not of the *jour*. No pretensions here. Must be just plain, solid good food.

New fast-food restaurants, three of them, opened nearby, as well as a fish and chips place, English style. These were followed by a Thai restaurant, and two serving pizza. And still Joe's Diner goes on. The prices? What people call decent. Still, other restaurants serve food at decent prices. It must be Joe's Diner, something special.

Finally, after years of wondering, I stop at the diner for a late breakfast. I move to the rear of the long counter and look at the menu. It is too late for regular breakfast and much too early for lunch. Breakfast at all hours, the sign on the wall says. I order eggs sunny-side, potatoes, toast and coffee. Then I look around. There is no Joe in sight, just two middle-aged women who look over-worked. Small wonder, since there is always someone eating here means that they are al-ways cooking and serving and picking up dishes.

Several newspapers have been left on the counter, testimony to all the people who have already stopped by that morning. I read a little of the news and sports as I wait to be served. Finally it arrives and I fold the news-paper in quarters so I may continue reading while I enjoy my meal.

Yetch! Yuck! Blotch. Blatt. Phooey. It is awful. Terrible. Blitch. Bluck. Patooey. Yetch again, and kapew. Double kapew!

How can anyone possibly ruin fried eggs? And toast? You call that butter? Coffee? *That* is coffee? Oh well, back to the crois-sants, the mandarin beef, or burritos, or Ar-gentine barbecue beef, or fish and chips, or a rich minestrone...or, maybe....a nice...won-ton soup....or....I know, there's a new East Indian restaurant that just opened down the street. I think I'll try it.

*Was it 1967? Oh, Hell, I don't remember.*

*I cross the country by train. The country is big. It is unbelievably beautiful to see the country from a train window. From Oakland, California, I go to Detroit for an annual meeting of the American Anthropological Association.*

*I cannot stand the excessively self-important tone of the papers presented. Even less can I stand the drinking parties at the hotel, working professionals acting like children. I take that back. It is an insult to kids. I understand other annual meetings for other associations are the same. Knowing this does not help. I feel alone in the crowd.*

*Lonely in Detroit, I check the yellow pages of the phone book. Restaurants. There it is: Mexican food. In Detroit? I go.*

*Tacos, enchiladas, guacamole, barbecued beef and pork, tortillas, humble beans, chocolate with cinnamon.*

*I eat alone in the restaurant, but I do not feel alone anymore. The loneliness is gone when I butter a nice, warm corn tortilla. Tomorrow I'm going to find a place that serves good breaded veal cutlets.*

# %

# THERE OUGHT
# TO BE A LAW

Like people everywhere, I watch the news on television and listen to it on the radio. I read newspapers and get information from magazines. And, to tell the truth, I can't resist reading at least a part of each newsletter that comes into my possession. In short, I am an avid information consumer.

It is because I am such a fanatical information consumer that I am constantly bombarded by percents. With fifty percent this, twenty-eight percent that, and two-hundred percent of something else, my life is inundated with percents. It seems that people are not people anymore. They are a high percent of this, and a low percent of that. There are so many percents in circulation that, as a result, I have become anti-percent. Enough is enough. There ought to be a law that protects the information consumer against the indiscriminate use of percents in the news.

In too many cases, a percent doesn't mean

a thing.  Just the other day I heard a radio news report in which it was claimed that the legal profession did not do enough to investigate and correct misconduct by lawyers. In response, someone speaking for the legal profession said that the accusation was not true.  "In fact," he went on to say, "our reprimands for misconduct by lawyers is up one-hundred percent above last year."  That was it.

Now, a one-hundred percent increase of anything certainly sounds terribly impressive.  And, in this case, a picture of great improvement was created.  But the person speaking for the legal profession did not give any concrete numbers, nor did the radio interviewer ask for them. So the listener is left in the dark.  News becomes non-news.

If you double something from one to two, you have increased it by one-hundred percent.  Four is a one-hundred percent increase if you began with two. The same applies to two-thousand or four-thousand.  In other words, although a one-hundred percent increase in reprimands sounded impressive, the speaker certainly said nothing, and information consumers got non-information.

Many colleges and universities disseminate information in this manner.  For example, institutions of higher learning systematically issue statements such as, "Our minority enrollment has increased by twenty percent this year." This creates a picture of considerable success, but what if the total number of students enrolled is eighteen thousand?

Watch out if the specific numbers are not provided for the consumer of information. After all, an increase of twenty percent of one-hundred-fifty is only thirty. This means almost nothing if the institution's entire enrollment totals eighteen thousand. One-hundred and eighty is a mere one percent of eighteen thousand. Therefore, what this institution has really said is that, "Our minority enrollment has now reached one percent of the total studentbody." Obviously, whoever gave out the information on minority enrollments decided that twenty percent is much more impressive than one percent!

Many social scientists are particularly fond of providing "scientifically impressive" non-information. For example, consider this statement recently made by a psychiatrist during a debate. "That is absolutely not true," he said, adding that, "Ninety percent of the studies indicate otherwise." Here we go again! Ninety percent? Of how many?

In the same vein, surveys by social scientists should be watched with extreme care. Consider this recent announcement by sociological researchers that "Hispanic males drink in excess." If you have the time to pursue the matter, soon you learn that the total sample in the study was twelve-hundred people. Of this number, fifty-two percent were White, twenty-eight percent were Black, and twenty percent were Hispanic. A little more calculating will tell you that twenty percent of twelve-hundred is two-hundred-forty. But, read on. You then discover that among the Hispanics in this study, sixty percent of them were male and forty percent female.

That leaves us with one-hundred-forty-four Hispanic males in the total sample. Now, presto and shazzam! We have witnessed the magic of sociological surveys. By looking at one-hundred-forty-four individuals, you then know how fourteen to fifteen million males will behave!

Maybe the survey professionals are trying to tell us something like, oh well, if you've seen one-hundred-forty-four Hispanic males, you've seen them all.

And, as if this were not enough to drive us information consumers out of our collective cotton-pickin' gourds, we must be wary when someone screams, "Budget cuts! Budget cuts! The sky is falling! Give us money." When a school principal or superintendent declares that utter disaster is around the corner because of "budget cuts," more often than not they are simply saying that they did not get the entire increase they wanted in the first place. For example, say they have requested a thirty percent increase, but they received twenty percent instead. The school people then tend to go public and announce in apocalyptic terms that they have suffered a ten percent budget cut! The actual increase is seldom mentioned, once again leaving the information consumer in the dark.

Perhaps in all of this I am only saying what consumers of information already know. And that is that a percent can be used to paint a rosy picture without actually giving out real information, as in the case of the news about

lawyers and universities outlined above.  Or,
a percent can be used to paint a picture of
impending doom, as in the example of the
"budget cuts." The case of the sociological
survey which used one-hundred-forty-four
persons to predict the behavior of some
fourteen to fifteen million people, of course,
is "science," and therefore beyond reproach
— except in the case of us alert consumers of
information.

*It is 1970.*

*I am forty-seven years old.*

*I run into an old friend.  I ask him about his family, his wife and children.*

*I always wonder if I should ask about them,because I know that he and his wife always seemed to be on the edge of leaving each other and taking the children, she from him, he from her.*

*Well, I blurt out, "I'm glad you two are still together."*

*"To tell the truth," he replies "when it comes right down to the nitty-gritty, agony crunch, I'm leaving her, she's leaving me, I can't take the kids from her, and she doesn't have the heart to take them from me.  For that, I will be forever grateful to her.  I hope she feels the same way."*

*"Ah, is this not love?" said the ancient Chinese philosopher.*

# KAELA

## 16 February 1920 – 15 August 1987

Kaela. What a pretty name. Born of Russian-Jewish immigrant parents. Dreams of a future. Kaela. She was a secretary at the School of Public Health, University of California at Berkeley, and more, one of that disappearing breed of university workers who take the meaning of a university to their hearts, who transcend the pettiness of separate departments and disciplines, who have gone far beyond the silly quarrels between the quantitative versus the qualitative, who have grown beyond the petulant prissiness between the rational and the intuitive, and who have introduced young people to the concept of love for what a university could and should stand for. It is a love that those students who knew her should carry with them for the rest of their lives, and they damn well better. Kaela. Secretary II, The University of California, Berkeley. Helper. A

natural intellectual with functioning tear
ducts. Poet. Human. Friend. Helper. Lover
of dictionaries and of words, using them
with a reverence and precision that was
humbling and enlightening. Disdain. Disdain
for those who didn't. Music. Vivaldi, Bach.
Food. Fresh asparagus, vine-ripe tomato,
juicy grapes, a plum. Ummmmmmm! Um!
Inheritor of the Great Liberal Traditions of
the Twenties, Thirties, and Forties. Disdain
for the right-wing opposition. Disdain also
for the subsequent mealy-mouthed liberalism. She was named Kaela. Kaela Petrov-
Reynolds. American.

Cancer.

One day, after diagnosis, she walked into
my office. Chemotherapy. Hair gone. Although all kinds of wigs were available, she
was wearing a kerchief on her head. For
walking, she used a cane. The kerchief
looked like a babushka. What a striking figure she presented for a woman who was dying. She was beautiful. I think she did it on
purpose, the babushka, the whole thing, I
mean. You have to have known Kaela to
think such a thought. How can I put it? She
exhibited a disdain that was acceptable, absolutely and totally acceptable. You know
what I mean? Her demeanor said that everything was, like, OK. I can still see her walk
proudly, if slowly, down the dark institution-
al hall, with her cane and her babushka, and
her head held very high. She had come to
say goodbye, to set us free. Thanks, Kaela. It
was a beautiful performance. Thanks for your
love.

Kaela Petrov-Reynolds. Secretary. Educator. Tough opponent. Very tough.

She knew the university. And who can possibly know how many manuscripts, for both faculty and students, were improved in style and content because of Kaela's editing and perceptive as well as analytical suggestions for improvement. (She would have hated the structure of this last sentence. Haven't I learned anything?)

One night, Mary called. "Kaela died," she said. "I know," I replied. "She said goodbye to me a couple of days ago." I didn't tell Mary that I hadn't seen Kaela for several months, but that I had clearly heard her voice. Mary and I talked a bit, then I said that I would light a candle for Kaela.

"I want to live long enough to see my grandchild who is on the way," Kaela had said. And she did. An inner light was in her eyes when she told me. Kaela lives.

Á Dios, Kaela. Rest In Peace.

But if you don't want to,

that's cool.

*It is 1971.*

*I am forty-eight years old.*

*We have lived in this neighborhood for two years.*

*I have taken to driving to work, going to the corner and turning right.*

*One morning, at the corner I see a woman cleaning the streets and sidewalks. She is about sixty-five years old. As she cleans, she loudly denounces all the people who have dropped their trash there. Her voice is angry. Apparently, she is what is called "mentally ill."*

*She is dressed in rags. Yet, she wants the street and sidewalks to be neat and orderly.*

*She becomes a regular, and I see her virtually everyday, busy, very busy, putting her world, our world, in order. No one cooperates, but she continues. The street corner is neat and orderly, that is to say, clean.*

*Then, one day, she is gone. Dead? Committed to an institution? Gone to another trashy city corner that needs cleaning more urgently?*

*I don't know.*

*But I still think of her.*

# ❶

# I GUESS I'LL NEVER BE
# A BIGSHOT

One day I went to a meeting concerning university business. Some twenty-five administrators and faculty were in attendance, and they droned on with talk of the business at hand. I say droned because I heard very little of the exchange of words. Instead, I spent the time of the meeting looking at the walls of the conference room, the chandelier, the long table, and at the floor.

The walls were beautiful, made of large and rectangular panels of light oak, smoothed to a touch similar to silk and brush-varnished so well that today, some fifty or more years later, the work still looked new. It was the work of master craftsmen. The wood grain was gold-white, and it was obvious that the panels had been selected and placed to form a harmonious symmetry, like the rings of a tree. The entire work was a testimonial of time beyond the original workers, as if they had wanted to talk to the future, to talk without words.

The fine art of the metal and glass workers had come together in the well-hammered chandelier, forming a graceful ring around which hung shining, many-faceted and softly angular icicles.

We all sat around an enormous conference table which, clearly, had been made about the same time as the walls and chandelier, and it had been made with the same craftsman-like care. Then a note of irritation swept over me when I noticed that someone had carved crude initials into the oak top. Others had made careless scratches and left messy ink blotches. Someone had destroyed the harmony here. The disfiguration triggered in me an urge to refinish the table top, to make it like new again. In that way, perhaps, I could somehow talk to the past and tell those workers...what?...tell them what?

The parquet floor was beautifully consistent with the walls, both in quality and careful work. It was difficult to imagine how the perfectly fitting pieces of wood had been cut with hand tools. The sanding must also have been done by patient hands. The floor was darker in color than the walls, possibly because of use and subsequent refinishing. I leaned over, pretending that I had dropped something, to touch the floor.

What...? What? Everyone at the table is getting up and leaving. The conference had been adjourned and I didn't even hear if we are to meet again. Near the door I turn and stop an acquaintance. "Look," I say, "Look at these walls, the woodwork. It's really something." He glances nervously at his watch and replies, "Can't stop now. I have another important committee meeting to go to."

"Well," I say to myself, "I guess I'll never be a bigshot." I turn and decide to remain alone in the room, to take more time to admire the very fine workmanship. To me, it is an enduring message from the past.

*It is 1974.*

*It is evening, and one of our two boys goes to our large refrigerator. He opens the door and leaves it open for a long time, looking at everything inside. The refrigerator is over-flowing with food of all kinds. Leaving the door open, he opens the freezer compart-ment. It, too, is full to the brim.*

*Then I hear, "Can we send out for pizza?"*

*"What do you want pizza for?" I reply.*

*"Because there's nothing to eat," he says. The tone of voice is so matter of fact that it carries an impression of absolute truth.*

*"What do you mean there's nothing to eat? The refrigerator is bulging with food!"*

*His face takes on a look of baffled pain.*

*He gets the pizza. Then he goes to bed.*

*School tomorrow.*

✧

# PEEPA CHICKEN

Take Peepa Chicken. She is hard to write about. See what I mean? Right away I am ending a sentence with a preposition. And, to make matters worse, now I've ended two sentences with a preposition.

"Waddle, waddle, waddle," That's what Branko used to say as Peepa Chicken walked around in her pen. Low-slung, Peepa walked somewhat like a duck. No offense meant to ducks. In fact, some of my best friends are ducks.

Here waddle, there waddle, everywhere waddle waddle. Peepa Chicken was a hen, eeya, eeya, oh. And in her nest she laid some eggs, eeya, eeya, oh.

She was always looking for geranium leaves and grapes, her favorite foods.

Araucana. That's what she was, a South American Araucana chicken. There are many, many kinds of chickens, but she was a very special Araucana. She had a beautiful voice, especially when she rushed to open-

133

ings in the chicken-wire to enjoy geranium leaves and grapes. I can still hear her musical voice. No, damn it, it was not a "cluck." Who in the name of historical hell dreamed up "cluck" for the sound of a chicken? Talk about sick people!

Camouflage. Her feathers were made to hide her, whereas Peepo the Rooster's feathers were not. He was gold and shining rust, she was a soft, golden, pale brown with camouflage spots on her neck and wings, like a wild bird. She would have been hard to find in a forest, or even in the open desert with its scant shrubbery in which to hide.

A red rose.

Peepa did not have a regular crest atop her head, like Rhode Island Red chickens. Instead, on her lower forehead, just above her beak, was a multi-layered round nub that looked just like a red rose. I've seen many other chickens, and none have had a red rose on their forehead. I used to feel irritated when some visitors did not notice Peepa's flower-crest.

As a boy it was my job to clean the chicken pen and coop, and I hated it! That's why initially I had told Branko he could not bring a couple of chicks home from his school. But I relented, and I fell in love with Peepa. She and Peepo became a part of our reality.

Cuddle. At night, on their roost made of a dry tree branch, Peepa and Peepo used to cuddle, roosting close to each other. I cannot recall ever going out there at night when she was not talking, while he just sat there silently. They were good friends, Peepa and

Peepo.  I used to visit them often.  It was
particularly good to see them after a difficult
day at work, very relaxing.  And I still laugh
when I think of the old feather mop Peepa
and Peepo had for a "mother" when they
were tiny chicks.

Again reality changed.  Peepa began to lay
eggs to hatch.  Her eggs were a pale bluish-
green, mottled with brown spots. Very pretty eggs.  She decided to have her brood away
from the coop, under a piece of plastic for a
roof, in an old table with cabinets underneath.  It was in the cabinets that she made
all her preparations. Peepa Chicken was very
busy now, going here and there. It was not
long before she had nine eggs in her nest.
Somehow, one broke, and she was left with
eight upon which to set and keep warm.

How long before chicken eggs hatch?
Twenty, twenty-one days?  Twenty-five days
passed by, and nothing. Then thirty. I wondered if her kind of chicken took longer.
Maybe. I'll give her a few more days.

For forty days and forty nights Peepa kept
her eggs warm.  Only rarely would she come
out to nibble a little, then she would dash
back to her nest.  Through bright sun,
cloudy days, cool nights and rain she sat
there, waiting, turning the eggs to keep the
temperature even.

On the fortieth day, Branko and I decided
to take matters into our own hands.  It was a
Saturday, and we drove to Napa, a rural area
north of Oakland.  There we found newborn
chicks at a farm supply center.  We bought
four Rhode Island Red chicks.

Returning home, we kept the chicks in the house where Peepa could not hear them. We waited until about midnight. Then we placed the chicks in a box and covered them with a towel to keep them quiet. Slowly we sneaked out to Peepa's nest, and even more slowly took the chicks one by one and placed them under Peepa, very gently. Immediately they scuttled under her feathers and began to peep happily. Peepa welcomed them with soft, motherly noises. I guess she was telling them that everything was all right in the world. "Tomorrow we'll know if she takes them," I told Branko.

Yep. She did. And an old board with small pieces of wood nailed across it made a fine ladder for the chicks to scurry in and out of their nest. Soon Peepa had them walking on the ground. She did what chickens do, took good care of them.

I had heard that roosters sometimes harm newborn chicks, so Peepa was kept separate from the rest of the pen. It was not long, however, before Peepo began to pace back and forth outside her enclosure, trying to get in. For her part, Peepa would pace back and forth, trying to get out. We decided to take a chance, even though the baby chicks were only a little over a week old. I opened the gate and Peepo walked in. He was gigantic next to the chicks. I watched for three hours, but I needn't have bothered. They all got along just fine.

Oh yes, the original eggs never did hatch. I disposed of them a few at a time, now that Peepa had taken to her new family of chicks.

Peepa was an attentive mother, certainly much better than a feather dust mop. But as the chicks grew bigger she became somewhat harsh with them, chasing them away when they came to eat with her. Maybe this was normal weaning, or perhaps she noticed that they were "different." With Peepa chasing the chicks around, and Peepo there, too, that pen was certainly a busy place.

All of them loved snails. Many times I've heard it said, "Let chickens or ducks loose in your yard, and you'll never have snails." On occasion I would lift an old board and take a special snail supper to the chickens. It wasn't long before the snail supply dwindled to practically none. That was when, one day, I raided the neighbor's ivy for snails. I only found a few, so I gave them to Peepa. It was a mistake. That evening I found her lying on the ground, trying to breathe as if her lungs were paralyzed. She didn't last long. "I'm so sorry, Peepa," I whispered to her, choking.

Later, I guessed, it was the snails from the neighbor's yard. They had had their yard systematically sprayed with a pesticide, something we would never do. The poison must have accumulated in the snails and that's what killed Peepa.

I felt bad. Such a pretty bird. Now here I am, several years later, still thinking of her. Years and years ago, when I was a very young boy who hated taking care of our chickens, who would have guessed that now I would choke up whenever I thought of one. But this one was different, she had a name.

Her name was Peepa Chicken.

**Golden Gate Park
San Francisco
It is 1975**


*I walk
through the park.*

*Tree leaves rustle in the breeze.*

*They absorb bird song,*

*absorb the rhythm*

*of a rabbit's heart flow.*

*The voices of people harmonize
with each other
with the song of the trees
the song of the birds
and
with the song in the rabbit's heart.*

♦

# PEEPO

His name was Peepo.

Today Peepo, the rooster, died. I held him as he opened one eye, then he was gone.

Once, when he was young and beginning to crow, a neighbor came to the door. He was a fiftyish urban man and very agitated. In surly tones he advised me that Peepo's crowing was bothering his wife, upsetting her considerably, not letting her rest and that she was a night-shift nurse. They lived a block away. In response I mumbled such words as motorcycles, loud trucks, airplanes, and teenagers racing noisy cars down residential streets, not to mention police, ambulance, and fire-engine sirens. This made him even more angry. "You'd better watch out," he scolded. "I'm a noise abatement officer and you'd better do something about that rooster."

"And I'm a psychiatrist who specializes in abnormal and sick people," I calmly lied.

The angry neighbor never came back. I wonder if he wondered if I was really a psychiatrist, just as I wonder if he was really a noise abatement officer for the city. I guess we'll never know. In any event, Peepo went on crowing but I didn't let him out of the enclosed coop until after breakfast.

Peepo used to talk to children. We live near a grammar school and each morning during the school year the children would walk by the house, five, six, seven and eight year olds talking, shouting, playing and arguing. When Peepo would hear them he would crow and crow and crow. The children would answer, imitating his call, and they would crow and crow and crow. They talked like this until there were no more children walking by the house.

Peepo's feathers. Light, shiny rust, holographic, turning to golden rust as the sun's rays reflected from them. Yellow, too. And white feathers. A very large and red crest, of course. A yellow-ivory beak, yellow, fish-scaled legs and feet and spurs. In our back yard in Oakland, Peepo was like a walking Aztec headdress, glimmering, graceful, and majestic.

"I want a boy chicken and a girl chicken," eight-year-old Branko Romano had said when his classroom hatched some eggs. Obviously the man who had volunteered to do this for the kids knew what he was doing, because that is exactly what Branko got. Who's to know? They were so tiny, and the two yellow fluffs looked alike.

Incubator hatched, their first "real" mother was an old feather dust-mop placed in a cardboard box (with a ticking clock to imitate a heart beat), in the kitchen. We all smiled when the tiny chicks relaxed and went to sleep under the protective cover of their mother-dust-mop, peeping softly as baby chicks do when they crawl under a mother hen.  That evening we named them Peepo and Peepa.

Peepo knew his territory and he protected it in the only way he knew, with focused fury.  One day I went into their pen to feed them.  They were now half-grown.  On this day, Peepo attacked with all the fury that a rooster can muster, which is a lot.  He drew blood through the thick cloth of my trousers.

With wings spread, his speed was surprising. He chased me out of the chicken pen.  I couldn't understand it.  He had always allowed me in to feed them.  The next day, and the next, he attacked.  Then he did not attack on a Saturday and a Sunday, but on Monday he did again.  That was when I figured out why.  During the week I had been wearing a new pair of shoes, rust colored. That evening I changed into my old pair and he did not attack.  The rust color of the new shoes was too much like the color of his feathers.  He must have thought I was another rooster.

Eventually, with a lot of talking, Peepo became used to the new shoes and allowed me into the pen without the need of the bamboo rake with which I would keep him at a distance. Now I remember that every time he had chased me out of the pen he had crowed and crowed victoriously.

Peepo was quite at home in his pen.  He wandered about, bathed in the soft dirt, and seldom bothered the wild birds that came to eat the chicken feed. Over time, mourning doves and sparrows made their pen a regular stop. Even blue jays would dart down for the sunflower seeds. Squirrels, too, scampered in and out, sometimes sitting near Peepo and Peepa with their tails twitching and their eyes peering about, always on guard for the appearance of our dog. Most striking of all the visitors to the pen were two pigeons, one a bright and pure white, its mate a shimmering dark gray, almost black. They were always together. I wondered which was the male and which was the female, and I found out when, one day, the dark gray pigeon was cooing with his wings slightly spread as he danced around the pretty white pigeon.

Even before Peepa had died, Peepo had developed a limp in his left leg. Perhaps one time when we were off on vacation someone taking care of the house kicked him when he attacked. Or perhaps he caught a spur on the wire mesh and twisted his leg. So now he limped along, left alone with the Rhode Island Reds that Peepa had raised.

About a year ago his limp got worse. Finally, he lost most of the strength in his leg and began to have trouble getting up. He would thrash about on the ground, making a lot of noise, until finally he could stand. It was very sad to see such a beautiful bird have to do that.

Then he stopped getting up altogether. His special diet, which we hoped would give him strength, had been peanuts, raisins, yellow cheese and lettuce, his favorites. I would hold a dish of water for him, and he would drink and drink. During those last few days he certainly drank a lot of water.

One morning Olga said, "I think you'd better check Peepo. He looks very stiff this morning."

I rushed out to the shed only in shirt, underwear and shoes, and I picked Peepo up. His neck was limp. I set him on my lap and began to talk, stroking the feathers behind his crest. Soon, he stiffened his neck enough to hold his head up, and he opened one eye halfway in response. I saw the black pupil. His iris was circled by a white and then a golden-orange stripe. I looked at him and he looked at me. As I began to set him down he made a slight noise, so I continued to hold him as he weakened more and more. Finally, he could hold his eye open no more, and I set him down in a bed of straw by the doorway.

A couple of hours later I was puttering around in the back yard and went in to check Peepo. One of the Rhode Island Red hens was setting toward the back of the coop, where she usually laid her eggs. This was the one that had taken to pecking and breaking her eggs. I left her long enough to lay her egg, and returned to retrieve it before any damage was done. She had moved and now she was sitting next to the still rooster. I left again, and shortly I heard her making soft noises, unlike any I had heard her or any chicken make before. I peeked in the door. She was standing atop a box next to Peepo, looking down at him and making a sad noise that was clearly a cry instead of a cluck. I looked down and there, next to his head with its closed eyes, was a fresh, warm, pale beige and slightly mottled egg.

The funeral was at one o'clock, Sunday, March 18th, 1984. Peepo was buried under the lemon tree, next to Peepa. He had a fresh straw bed to lie on, with some grapes, chicken feed, and peanuts, shelled. Beside him was a copy of Branko's book of chicken cartoons which had been inspired by Peepo and Peepa. And next to Peepo's head I gently placed the egg which the chicken had laid not long before as she sat next to him. It was the first egg in a long, long time that she had not cracked open with her beak right after laying it.

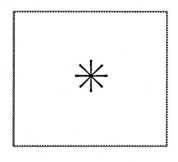

*It is the late Seventies.*

*I am in my late fifties.*

*I am lecturing to a class of graduate students. It is clear I am leading up to a major point.*

*In the back row sits Hermán, a student from Costa Rica. He has his handkerchief out, but he is holding back. He doesn't want to be rude and blow his nose while I am speaking.*

*I finish lecturing and ask a question of the class. During the ensuing silence, Hermán takes the opportunity to blow his nose. It is heard throughout the classroom, but no one says or does anything until I say, "No, Hermán, that is not the right answer."*

*The class breaks out into laughter.*

*Hermán, thinking they are laughing at him, defends himself as best he can.*

*"It may not be the right answer, Professor," he retorts, "but it sure is the right sound track for the lecture."*

*Half the class is uncomfortable, while the other half guffaws.*

*If I recall correctly, my laughter was the loudest.*

# THE SILENCE

By rural standards, our back yard is not large at all. By crowded city standards, however, it is bigger than many apartments. Almost a fourth of it is covered by a garage originally built for the smaller cars of the 1920's. And about a half of the yard was cemented over before we moved in, a basketball court for children. At the edge of the cement grows a lemon tree, a very pretty lemon tree. It offers fruit all year long. Behind the lemon grows a small lime tree. It, too, offers its fruit all year long.

Under the lime tree, sometimes twice a day, I scatter wild bird seed which I purchase at one of the two local supermarkets. Noisy sparrows, soft-sounding mourning doves, domineering blue jays, and a husband-wife pair of pigeons daily arrive to eat on the uncemented ground. On occasion, an escaped parakeet joins in the fare. Squirrels that live nearby join the birds, deftly splitting the sunflower seeds which the birds do not eat. Sometimes there is a fierce compe-

tition between the squirrels and the blue jays
to see which gets to the sunflower seeds
first, or which gets the most. The birds, especially the sparrows, dart away quickly to a
nearby tree, and return just as quickly. By
comparison with the always calm pigeons,
they are in a constant state of nervous activity.

Near the spot where the birds eat, three
bright green celery plants are growing. Have
you ever tasted home-grown celery? What it
does to a soup or a casserole borders on the
miraculous. Use only about one-third as
much as the store-bought because home-
grown is not insipid.

The birds do not bother the celery. But
some of them peck away at the small cabbage
plants. Apparently they have not found cabbage to their liking because the plants are
still there. Nor have they bothered the cauli-
flower. The lettuce is something else. Fool-
ishly, I tried to grow some succulent lettuce
right there in front of all those birds. I guess
the birds think that baby lettuce borders on
the miraculous. Oh well, probably there are
some people in the world who think it is
right and proper to plant something special
that the birds can eat. After all, who wants
to eat seeds all of the time?

Against the white wall of the garage,
where the sun will reflect warmly, three
young grape vines are ending their winter
dormancy as they replicate in chlorophyll
the brightening light of spring. From their
dead-looking stalks, yellowish buds push out.
They must make grapes. It is an imperative.

A pear and a nectarine tree are in full bloom. Pink nectarine blossoms space themselves along the still bare branches, and the pear tree has become a bouquet of crowded clusters of white flowers. Bees are busy there, even though it is somewhat late in the afternoon. Bees in the city? All of my life I have seen bees, but at this moment it seems I have seen them for the first time. Have you ever done that? You see something almost everyday of your life, then all of a sudden it is as if you have never seen it before. I smile inside. Magically, I fall in love with those bees, and I want to tell the world. I want to make a television documentary about bees in the urban environment, in back yards, front yards, church and school yards, along the sloping sides of freeways as autos blindly whiz by, in empty lots (Why do people call empty lots 'empty lots'? They're not empty).

With a documentary on bees in the city I would surely break new ground because nature documentaries always seem to deal with places far away, where few if any people actually live.

I am home from work. I scatter bird seed. I hear the birds but I don't see them. They are waiting in nearby trees. I sit and watch as the sparrows are first to arrive. They streak to the fence, then to the lime tree, and to the ground. Tiny, tiny seeds. Somehow they break them open and eat only the inside kernel. Furiously, they peck away and peck, dart away and return, over and over. The mourning doves arrive. Briefly they sit along the edge of the garage, or on the fence, patiently waiting until all is clear. Food can mean danger to animals and birds in the wild. Maybe it is the same with people. I think it is. High atop our two-story house a gray pigeon has been watching. It joins the other birds. Next to the sparrows, the pigeon looks gigantic. There is constant bird noise as the seed supply dwindles.

It is the third calendar day of spring, and there are about fifty birds eating on the ground. More wait in the trees. They eat about forty pounds of seed each month. It costs less than a fifth of decent brandy. When it rains hard there are no birds. Later in the year, when the little ones have hatched and are learning to fly, I will see their mothers bring them to the place of unending seeds. There, the mothers will pick up a seed and place it in the beak of the little ones. Apparently they are good teachers. There are many sparrows.

Watching them is almost my daily ritual in the sanctuary of my back yard. The music of the birds is soothing. Suddenly, the pigeon unexpectedly flies away rapidly, flapping its wings in an unusually loud fashion. Normally, it merely flies away in a leisurely manner when it is done eating. Moments later, the mourning doves begin to leave just as rapidly. I am on alert. This is doubly unusual. Suddenly, there is a mixture of doves and sparrows in the air all at once. From the side of the house, behind me where I cannot see, probably from high atop the American elms across the street, a pair of wings, gray and white blurs, swoosh down under the lemon

tree and curve up to a tall pine as simultane-
ously I hear the distraught and piercing
shriek of a mortally wounded sparrow. A
hawk? I look up. It is gone, as quickly as it
appeared. From above, I see something small
slowly floating down. It is a tiny, gray feather.

Then there is silence. It is an enormous
silence. Not a bird is in sight. The silence
envelopes everything. I stare at the remaining bird seed, look up and back as the silence continues. The sparrow is gone. Later, the others will return, but I do not wait. I
leave my sanctuary and return inside the
house.

It is almost six o'clock now. I don't think
the death of this little bird will make the
evening news. Then, I think one of those
thoughts.

*"Good evening. I'm Dan Rather, and this
is the CBS Evening News. Today, according
to a highly placed government official, world
arms control still seems to be a remote possibility, but very remote. In Boston, an apartment fire has killed six people. Elsewhere,
in India, protests increase over government
policies, while two more casualties have
been reported in Ireland's unending war.
Meanwhile, in Oakland, California, a sparrow
has died in the claws of what one local ob-
server believes was a hawk. These stories
and more, when the news continues."*

*It is 1981.*

*I say to twelve year old Branko, "Don't forget to do your math homework tonight."*

*"I don't have to do it. I already know it," he replies with supreme assurance.*

*"How do you know you know it if you haven't done it?"*

*"I just know I know it."*

*"All right, if you know so much, give me an answer to this problem and I'll give you a quarter."*

*"OK."*

*"What's seven times nine?"*

*"Forty six!"*

*"That's the wrong answer. You don't get the quarter."*

*"Well, you didn't say it had to be the right answer!"*

*P.S.   He got the quarter.*

¿

# SELF-ESTEEM

As of March, 1987, the State of California
has its very own official State Commission on
Self-esteem. Its mission? To seek and destroy low self-esteem wherever it may be
found.

The Commission is also expected to produce new and improved self-esteem. Whose
self-esteem will they improve? That of the
politicians? Nope. They were the ones who
voted to fund the Commission in the first
place. Perhaps they could focus on improving the self-esteem of those legislators who
voted against the bill. Nope. Too petulant.
People with high self-esteem, which I'm
sure all fifteen or twenty members of the
Commission have, are not supposed to engage in petulant behavior that is obvious. Bad
for the image.

Well, then, whose self-esteem can they
improve? Bank executives? No. Too politically powerful. Besides, no one has proven
that bankers have low self-esteem. Good
idea for a hefty research grant here, though.

Who else? University professors? No, again. Everyone knows that university professors have very high self-esteem, whether warranted or not. Well, then, how about the self-esteem of public school teachers. Now, there is a possibility. After all, teachers say they are underpaid and overworked, and therefore held in low esteem by nearly everybody including the public, the legislature, and the governor. This, we are told, has a negative effect on teachers' self-esteem, and it has led to most of the deficiencies in the education of our children. The solution is simple. In fact, it is so simple that I plan to submit it to the Commission. I'm surprised no one has thought of it before.

The solution to our educational problems is to overpay the teachers. Yes. Overpay them by so much that their individual and collective self-esteem inevitably will rise sky high. Then we'll have the best public schools ever. And we will have the most studious, productive, and happy students in the world, each with a very high self-esteem because the size of their classes has been reduced in the process.

Let's see, on whom else could the Commission focus? The Teamsters? Brrrrr! County supervisors? Members of the Society for the Prevention of Cruelty to Animals? No. But wait, how about cats and dogs? Now there's an idea. The Commission could work in tandem with animal psychiatrists, of which there is a steadily growing number. Think of all the employment possibilities. Where to begin? With the dogs and cats that

belong to the wealthy?  No.  Everybody
knows that those animals have a very high
self-esteem, indeed, what with all those ped-
icures, highly professional hairdos, per-
fumes, ribbons, and unlimited health care.

Then, how about the cats and dogs of the
middle class?  Dangerous ground, there, especially with the growing resentment by the
middle class toward government interfer-
ence.  That leaves us with the cats and dogs
of the poor people.  There must be a lot of
those.  And surely the pets that belong to
poor people must have a very low self-
esteem.  I mean, it stands to reason!

But, what if there are too many?  The
Commission must begin somewhere.  Why
not begin with the cats and dogs that belong
to people whose annual income is less than
$17,000?  Oops.  That group may be too
large for the Commission to handle.  Wait.
How about focusing on the dogs and cats that
belong to poor people earning less than
$17,000 yearly and who live in urban areas?
Yes.  Possible.  The target population can be
refined even more.  Good thing there are pet
psychiatrists around.

Money is scarce these days.  We have to
limit ourselves constantly.  Well, then, how
about a pilot project beginning with the cats
and dogs of urban people who earn under
$17,000 per year, who belong to a minority
group, in which at least one member of the
family is alcoholic, and one child has
dropped out of high school, and another
child is rebellious in grammar school?  Yes,
yes, that's it!

It will take at least one year to identify and locate this target population. By then, the Commission will have to go to the legislature and ask for monies for the second year. Shucks, just getting started in a real breakthrough, and now they need more money. Anything less, clearly, will be harmful to the self-esteem of the Commission members themselves. Ye gads, what if the Commission is not refunded at all? This could be devastating to the members, and they could all end up with an extremely low self-esteem.

Certainly this would be most embarrassing to the California State Legislature, which funded this project. But, then again, can legislators actually be embarrassed by anything? No. Why not? Because, actually, they have no self-esteem, neither low nor high. Otherwise, politicians wouldn't do what they do. Ego? Yes. Self-esteem? No.

And that is the problem.

I think that when the California State Legislature funded a State Commission on Self-Esteem, it was a subconscious cry for help.

*It is 1987, but within my mind it is 1933.*

*Our family goes to visit distant relatives who live in the mountains of Baja California. It takes three hours on rutted dirt roads to travel sixty miles.*

*They give us a jar of honey from their bee-hives. We give them a gallon of coal oil brought from the city. Now they can have light at night.*

*On the way home, we stop by a creek. The women step out to pick wild mustard greens, watercress, and blackberries. My uncle looks around and leaves with his shot-gun. We wait patiently, while we eat the ber-ries. Soon, he returns with two rabbits.*

*That evening, we have rabbit (fried in a batter made with eggs from our chick-ens), mustard greens and watercress. We pick fresh mint from our garden and drink mint tea sweetened with our gift of honey. Dessert is a slice of fresh orange. It has been a good day. Conversation during the entire dinner is softly musical.*

*Fifty-five years later, in 1987, I am having dinner at a Chinese restaurant in northern California. It is served with a slice of bright fresh orange.*

*I look at the beautiful fruit and I remem-ber that day, long ago.*

# THE PHONE CALL

The spring sun lingered on the horizon long enough to paint the clouds, hills, trees and west-facing windows all over the city. You know the colors. You've seen those sunsets, the kind that invite you to look again, and again, until finally you look one more time and it is gone.

I had taken our two dogs, Peppy the mother, and Xerox her son, for a customary walk. They are both small black dogs. Xerox got his name because he looks like his mother. Many people cannot tell them apart. We had gone to the grounds of the Dominican seminary across the street where the dogs can run between a row of heavily-leafed poplars on the east, and a row of sparse, delicately leafed elms on the west. On the northern side of the grounds enormous American elms were still waiting for the very end of the spring season before filling the air with such a profusion of foliage that they attract people for miles around. To the south, an equally tall ponderosa pine continues to grow according to its own clock.

I throw a red rubber ball and Peppy furiously runs after it, snap-grabs it tightly with a single chomp of her strong jaws, turns, then drops it limply with supreme indifference, not even bothering to look at the ball again. Xerox is somewhat different. True, he runs furiously after the ball and catches up to it. But he does not chomp on it. Instead, he makes a graceful turn and runs off to sniff a tree, perhaps there to lift a small, black rear leg.

Each time they abandon the ball I go after it, grab it and, because humans are obviously smarter than dogs, I throw it again. I guess at this point I could make the old joke that the dogs actually run me, but the truth of the matter is that we run each other. During these moments, we are a pack.

We return home, careful of the cars passing by our house. Peppy has already been hit once. Xerox jumps and rolls happily in the neighbor's ivy. I throw the rubber ball and Peppy catches it in mid-air, carries it a few feet and drops it again. We repeat this several times. It is the law of the pack. I throw, she drops.

Inside, Olga has filled the rooms with the fragrance of meat, herbs, and cooking vegetables. There is no exhaust fan above the stove, so we are not strangers to the smells of dinner. In this day of high-tech, mostly the poor, it seems, have this luxury left to them, when they have something to eat, that is.

Upstairs, older son Chico is working on college computer science homework, or on introductory philosophy. Downstairs, in the living room, younger son Branko is working on health, history, or English literature, while not answering the incessant phone calls from his high school friends. I go out the back door to scatter bird seed, check the peach, pear, nectarine and apricot trees, one of each. The prickly pear cactus has young, tender leaves ready for cutting, draining and cooking. They taste somewhat like raw string beans. As I glance down the driveway I see several people dragging themselves home from work in San Francisco, Berkeley, and other surrounding communities. They work hard, or their work is hard on them. I can see it in their faces. I try not to think about it because such thoughts are not for the evening sanctuary of my back yard.

It is almost dinner time when I return inside. Branko is on the phone talking to one of his friends. Olga is waiting there, to tell him dinner is ready. Branko is saying, "B.J. has had an accident." He holds his hand over the mouthpiece. "He was on a motorcycle, a car hit him." B.J. is also one of his school friends. "He's at the hospital, on a machine. He's hurt real bad, and he's in a coma." Olga exclaims and her eyes cloud over. Mine cloud over, too. A kid. Just a kid! Seventeen. Only seventeen. My God.

Visions of the worst disturb our minds, an extended coma, paralysis. We return to what we had been doing, seemingly normal, but I know that, even as we move about, Olga and I are praying. I didn't know him at all, and she had seen him only once or twice. But, at this moment of crisis, it is as if we had known this boy forever.

The next morning we learned more. Hospital trauma unit. Several doctors, all night long. Intersection. Dragged under a car. Motorcycle. No helmet, which had been stolen. But, after all, it was a ride of only a few blocks. Extreme heat of catalytic converter burns shoulder severely. Fractures, face, ribs, legs. Heavy loss of blood. Transfusions. Had the trauma unit not been nearby, he probably would have died. Had the accident happened in most any other country, he surely would have. And, if it had happened here just ten or twenty years ago he would not have lived. Two days later, his vital signs are good, but he has not opened his eyes.

If this were rural Mexico, I would have composed a *corrido*, a ballad, about this kid. And perhaps future generations would sing about him and thereby warn others about danger. But the ballad is unborn, and I am left with the memory of a suffering teenager, and a distinct empathy for his parents in their agony.

After dinner, teenage Branko is leaving for the library, and to visit friends. I stop him at the door. "What?" he asks, with a note of impatience in his voice. "Be careful," I say to him. And from the next room the voice of his mother is heard, "Be home early! School day tomorrow. And, Branko, be careful."

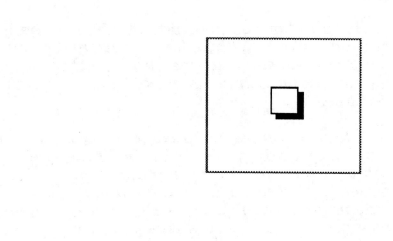

*It is an early afternoon in 1987.*

*I park the car down the street. Parking is getting worse in our neighborhood. I am irritated even though this is a minor matter. What does it hurt to walk about 150 feet? As I approach our home, a suspicious character walks quickly out of the driveway. He is about six-feet tall, thin, dressed like a hiker, very light brown, long hair and moving briskly. There have been recent burglaries, so I am downright angry, as would be any self-respecting man who is protecting his home.*

*"What are you doing in our driveway?" I demand loudly. "I will call the police. You have no business on our property! Who are you?"*

*He is a Norwegian student, about twenty-one years old. With a heavy accent he tells me he is traveling around the world, walking mostly; India, China, Mexico, Peru, the United States.*

*"I had an empty soda can," he explains. "I saw your garbage cans in the driveway. I didn't want to throw my garbage in the street." But I am wise to the ways of the city. I demand identification. He shows me his passport. Later, still suspicious, I check the garbage. On top of the trash there is an empty aluminum can. We do not drink that brand of soda at home. He was legit.*

*New Yorkers would have been proud of me. Never trust anyone. Dislike everyone. No matter what, always be mad.*

◻

# AFFIRMATIVE ACTION

A lot has been written about affirmative action, and considerable effort has been devoted toward this end to bring equity to more segments of our society, particularly for the minorities. Still, there are many people who say that the overall effort has been considerably less than successful, and much remains to be done.

This being the case, sometime ago I decided to seek a solution to the problem, wherever it may exist. But what could I do? All kinds of people have contributed their talents toward this end; lawyers, teachers, executives, students, legislators, and many others. How could my efforts come up with anything that has not been tried previously?

After considerable thought about the matter, I was almost ready to quit trying when, all of a sudden, the solution was right there in front of me. And, of all places, it was in the sports pages of the local newspaper. Well, the solution for affirmative action was not really there, but the idea was, and I wondered why no one had thought of it before.

The newspaper's sports pages carried a story about a midwest small college football coach whose football team had lost 126 games in a row. And the team's coach was not even from what is known as an ethnic minority. "That's it!" I thought with elation. "That's the solution. Hire a minority coach to lose that many games!"

Then, dammit, the doubts set in. I felt a gnawing fear that we could not find an His-panic, Black, Asian, or Native American who would be qualified. "Where can we find a mi-nority coach who can equal this accomplish-ment?" I asked myself. Perhaps we could find a Chicano coach who could lose thirty, forty, maybe even eighty consecutive football games. But to lose 126???

Well, perhaps with some intensive reme-dial education the potential minority coach could be taught to lose that many games. But he'd have to want to, I mean, really want to. After all, don't people say you have to aim high if you want to accomplish anything? Pick a role model and try to be like that per-son, they always say.

Are there other such role models? I think so.

Not too long ago, for example, a major American corporation reported a loss of 410 million dollars in one fiscal year. "Aha! In the interest of true affirmative action," I thought, "why can't we find a minority per-son to lose 410 million dollars in twelve months?" When prorated, that comes to a little over thirty-four million in losses per month. Lives there a minority somewhere in this nation who can measure up to this accomplishment?   Then, the doubts again. Maybe training for this should begin in high school. (There are some who believe that this process has already begun in our public schools.) Perhaps what the minorities would need in order to measure up in this regard is more compensatory education, or one of those special programs for the culturally deprived.

After all, not having the opportunity to bankrupt a multi-million dollar corporation is certainly a form of cultural deprivation.   If it isn't, then I don't know what is.

Maybe there's a cultural barrier somewhere in there.   Maybe it's genetic. Maybe it is a question of the minorities' DNA.   Perhaps with proper genetic engineering....

Or, perhaps all this could be resolved by intensive exposure of minority kids to the life of Ernest Breech.   Who is Ernest Breech, you ask?   He was president of the Ford Motor Company in 1948 and was reported to have said of the Volkswagen, "That car is not worth a damn."   Instead, we got the Edsel.

I say Blacks have just as much right to invent an Edsel as anybody else.   So do the Paiutes, and the Navajos.

The world of book publishing is an excellent field for the training of promising minority interns on how to emulate non-minority editors.

Here, the trainees could study the process by which twenty-one publishers rejected *M.A.S.H.*, eighteen turned down *LORNA DOONE*, another eighteen publishers also rejected *JONATHAN LIVINGSTON SEAGULL*, twenty publishing houses rejected *KON-TIKI*, and sixteen turned down *THE PETER PRINCIPLE*.

Surely we could scout throughout the minority communities and find people who can be trained to reject such works as these. Give them a chance, I say. Perhaps, if our efforts are successful, we could find some ghetto kid who could grow up to bankrupt an airline, thereby fitting right in with much of what is happening today in the mainstream.

For a training ground for minorities in this new and improved affirmative action, I suggest San Jose, California. The management of this city is quite experienced. Recently, for example, that growing city totally lost $60,000,000 of its investments. Poof! Just like that, and there went sixty-million of the public's money down the tubes, lost, alles kaput, adios dinero del publico (ah-dee-os dee-ney-roh dell poo-blee-coh). And this happened not long after the San Jose Unified School District declared bankruptcy in spite of yearly increases in public funding. It sure is clear that the city government of San Jose makes that football coach who lost 126 consecutive games look like a rank amateur.

Like all great breakthroughs in history, however, my new and improved affirmative action has its drawbacks. In our zeal for equality, should we encourage future minority scientists to invent such things as Thalidomide, DES, the swine flu vaccine, or intrauterine devices that puncture and cause serious infections, sometimes sterility?

Whatever the case may be, I think the time is ripe for a sweeping revision of our affirmative action policies. After all, each one of us should keep in mind that every year we have a holiday to celebrate and honor the man who discovered this land, a man who, as we are all aware, did not even know where he was.

It is February 1, 1987, 5:30 PM, and the days are getting longer.

I cross the street again. I am walking the dogs again. It is cold, so I zip up my fishing jacket.

The sun is low on the horizon, but I cannot see it because of buildings and trees. Still, the familiar evening glow shines about thirty feet above the ground.

I turn and look eastward at a straight row of poplar trees. At this time of year they are leafless. A few years ago, the poplars were topped. Now, there is a myriad of small shoots inching ever upward above each tree. The late sun shines on the shoots. From a distance, they are a golden beige.

Behind the beige-colored shoots are dark gray clouds.

Beige on gray.

It is beautiful beyond word description, beyond an artist's painting, beyond photography, and beyond computers.

Since I cannot describe it, paint it, photograph it, or computerize it, I pause long enough to etch the sight into my mind and into my soul.

Then, I continue walking the dogs, just like nothing has happened.

# THE HOUSE
# ACROSS THE STREET

I practice the custom of watching, just like in the old days. I'm always watching something, or somebody. On a bus, I watch the passengers. In restaurants, I watch the customers. At cocktail parties, I watch the guests. And at home, I watch the neighborhood. As often as possible, I'm near a window, watching what is happening outside.

That's how I came to watch David Helman, his wife Margot, and their four children, neighbors who used to live across the street from us in another neighborhood. They had lived in their modest and very unkempt house for some ten years. So little attention did the Helmans give to their house that the window sills hardly had any paint remaining on them. It was the same with the walls which were covered with dozens and dozens of peeling strips of paint. Grass of several varieties and many generations covered their yard, front, back, and sides. Each year fresh, newly green, grass grew to cover the brown dead remains of the previous year's growth. Strips of grass also covered the many cracks in their crumbling cement driveway.

I watched the Helman house deteriorate for many years. It was a slow process. "A blot on the neighborhood," I used to mumble, remembering when the Helmans moved in. Their house had been freshly renovated, the garden was lush with flowers, and the cement in the driveway was smooth and even. I'm sure that is why they bought it, everything was so well taken care of that all they had to do was provide the furniture. But many years had passed and, clearly, they had done very, very little to keep their house even in reasonably good shape. Yes, I was right, "A blot on the neighborhood."

Can you imagine my great surprise when, one Saturday morning, I resume my custom of watching and see David Helman, himself, busily cutting and pulling the weeds in his front yard? What? He had a hoe, rake, a shovel, and a shiny red wheelbarrow. All were new.

He worked all day, and it must have been very hard on him because he was an office worker during the week. Then came surprise number two when I saw his two sons come around the side of the house with garbage bags full of the weeds they had been pulling in the back yard. I had never seen the two sons do anything around the house— I mean, for the house. Together they filled a small truck they had rented and hauled the load off to the dump.

The next morning I was awakened by a loud, pounding noise, sledge hammer blows cracking the driveway cement on what should have been a nice, quiet Sunday. But it was not to be because David Helman and his two sons were hard at work again, cracking big chunks and little pieces of cement and loading them on the truck. All day they worked, just as they had on Saturday. By evening the driveway was clear of cement and they were smoothing the ground, setting lines of string. It was obvious that soon a new driveway would appear there, a smooth and welcoming driveway, just as it had been when they moved into their house.

On Monday morning, Helman went to work at his usual hour. During that day, his sons sort of tinkered at removing flakes of paint from the walls and window sills. That evening, however, when the father returned, the work tempo quickened as the three scraped, sanded, and prepared the walls for fresh paint. Soon, even Mrs. Helman and daughters joined in the work. It was pleasant to see an entire family working together that way. More families should do things together, especially when it comes to fixing up the house where they live.

As I watched during the following days, the Helman house was undergoing a steady transformation. "The rebirth of a house," I called it, a return to an earlier day, only better now with the dedicated work of that family. They even had a healthy argument, there in the front yard, over the color they were going to paint the house. The mother and daughters won, and soon there appeared a house painted with gleaming white enamel and trimmed with a rich, navy blue. The painting coincided with the first blooms of

the newly planted garden. It was almost unbelievable what four people could do once
they had set their minds to it.

I was happy for the Helman family, and
the wonderful thing they were doing. A new
driveway, a new garden, a new lawn, and
now a newly painted house. It must have had
a salubrious effect on them, too, for one day I
saw the eldest son scrubbing away a few
drops of oil that had dripped from the family
car onto the driveway's new cement. A bit
excessive, I thought at the time, but certainly forgivable when one takes pride in a task
well done. However, I thought they all went
to an unnecessary extreme when I noticed
they had altogether stopped using their new
driveway and began to park their car in the
street. Well, it should wear off soon, just like
the nervousness one feels about a new car
and not wanting a scratch or a nick on it.
Perfectly understandable.

Paneling. Pretty new wall panels for the
Helman house. Tied with ropes atop the
family car, they were carefully unloaded and
carried inside. Then came a truck and crew
from the National Floor Company, followed
by a new stove and refrigerator after the new
floor had been put in. I fully expected a
truck load of furniture, but none came. I
surmised that they had exhausted their re-
sources. No matter. How proud they must
be of their work. In just ten weeks they had
undone ten years of deterioration. Now, before my eyes, there was a gleaming, renovated house which could well become the
showcase of the entire street. I think every-

one was happy for the Helman family. Someday, perhaps, with a little time and money I
could renovate our home in that manner.
Probably other neighbors on the street were
thinking the same thing. A thought flashed
across my mind. What if the entire street
followed the example of the Helman family?
What a beautiful street this would be!

I had actually made plans and priced
items when, one day, I noticed a car park in
front of our home. A well-dressed man
emerged and walked across to the Helman
house. He was inside for a few minutes, after
which he walked out and hammered a sign
into their new lawn.

HOUSE

## FOR SALE

**BAY SITES REALTY**

*SPECIALISTS
IN RENOVATED HOMES.*

*It is 1987.*

*I receive a chain letter.*

*It says that if I send out 20 copies of the same letter, immediately, to 20 different people, I will receive great wealth. If I don't, something bad will happen to me.*

*I do not send out 20 copies.*

*That same day, I purchase a lottery ticket. The top prize is $14,000,000.*

*I don't win.*

*The chain letter was right.*

*Not winning $14,000,000 is a bad thing to have happen to me, especially at my age.*

# LET'S FIGHT!

Every now and then I feel like taking on the whole world. And that's how I feel right now. So let's have at it. Get ready, because I'm coming at you right now.

If you are one of those people who is so compulsive that you have to totally finish fixing up your back yard, you have been, and are, missing one of the ultimately supreme joys in the entire world. And it's your fault for being so uncontrollably shortsighted and compulsive in the first place.

OK. I've never met anyone who agrees with me on this, but why should that change my mind? It just convinces me that the world is full of people who are helpless and driven beyond all rationality, that's all.

Just think, if you finish fixing up your back yard, then you become a caretaker rather than a creator. Your work becomes maintenance, and remains just mechanical maintenance. You become a slave. You work your butt off just to keep the place looking the same. You become a rote person. Rote, by the way, means "routine or repetition carried out mechanically and without any understanding." Is that what you want to be for the rest of your life? So you plant Violets, instead of the Petunias of last year. Big, big deal.

Listen to me. Never, never finish fixing up your back yard. It's the worst thing you can do. Don't be a rote repeater. Be a creator. Think about it. If you go to bed at night without having finished the back yard, then you can plan, have visions of beauty, visions of an ever-changing landscape, visions of the eventual fulfillment of your dreams, someday, maybe tomorrow. You do this, and you go to bed a creator, not a rote repeater.

Not only that, but suppose you have a few leisure moments. Take a drink and sit on the back porch. You can't sit on the patio chairs because you are still planning what kind to get, or make, and where to put them, either on the ground or on the deck you are planning to build, or have built.

See what I mean? No, don't interrupt. I'm trying to tell you that I have planned some of the most beautiful and creative decks in the world, and I have done all this while simply sitting on my back— porch, that is. But wait. What good is a deck? It covers the ground and you can't plant anything unless it is in pots. There, you see? If you finish a deck in your back yard, then you have limited your options for creative planning and you're stuck with going to bed at night with nothing to look forward to but maintaining the deck. What is so hot about that? I say, and I can't say this forcefully enough, *"Don't finish that deck!"*

Don't finish anything in that back yard. Keep it alive. Keep it changing. Keep it in tune with the finest of your dreams. Back yards are like humans. What would happen if humans stopped changing at age three? See what I mean? It stands to reason if you just think about it. Let your back yard grow. Let it grow along with you. Don't stifle it in its prime. Let it serve your needs of today. Of course it can't do this if you have stopped growing. Have you? Has a finished back yard turned you into a mechanical and robotic maintenance wimp? Well, you know what they say, people are known by the company they keep. I say, people are known by their back yards. They're either wimps or they're not.

There may be one exception to what I am trying to tell you, which is when you are going to sell your house, along with its unfinished back yard. Check out your potential buyers for possible wimpishness. If they test positive, then rush out and hire someone to finish, I mean totally finish, fixing up your back yard so that there is nothing, absolutely nothing, left to plan for or do. The wimps then, in groveling gratefulness, will pay a premium price.

Everybody has cousins. Don't they? I have cousins. I have one particular cousin, and he has taken the very same attitude toward his house that I have toward my back yard. My cousin's house has never been finished, and he has been working at it for over forty years!

Every time you visit their house, his house, it is different. Sometimes it is a little different, sometimes very different. That house is not a structure. It is an organism. It grows. It shrinks. It reacts to the vicissitudes of everyday life. It reacts to dreams and to failures. It also tells you when nothing is happening. It gives and it takes. It is a part of the collective family. One day it is the backdrop for a small business, the family retreating to the rear so that the work can take place where the public can see it and come to purchase goods. The next day it is a restaurant. The family does not retreat this time, for he has built an addition with a few small tables. Then, you visit again. There is an indoor fountain, and people enjoy dining to the sound of trickling water, trickling onto growing goldfish. Then, the rear quarters of the restaurant become the study hall of ambitious college students, who happen to be their growing daughter and her boyfriend. *Voila!* And before you can say *"Voila!"* the rear of the restaurant has become nuptial quarters. The house grows, or the house shrinks. And my cousin, he grows and shrinks along with it. Such a business!

Like I was telling you, don't ever finish your back yard. If you do, you're dead. And if you think you can re-do heaven, you've got another think coming. Planning time is over, buddy.

Tomorrow I'm going to plant some carrots. I hope this time I'll have better luck with my plans. Last time they grew all crooked in the clay soil, and among a lot of weeds. Still, crooked carrots in a weed patch taste as good as the perfectly straight ones you can buy at the supermarket, maybe better.   Yes, very much better.

What a nice plan.  I can taste those carrots already.   Tonight I'll sleep real good— start first thing tomorrow, for sure.

ZZZZZZZ..................

*It is 1987.*

*In your mind, picture, if you will, a sunflower.*

*Chances are that your mind has reproduced a sunflower that is large, with bright yellow sun petals around the edge. In the full-bodied center, a dense profusion of seeds crowd each other. When mature, the seeds will splash onto the ground, there to gamble with nature.*

*It is also the picture of a sunflower that children carry in their minds.*

*Picture now, a flowerpot. It is but eight inches across and ten inches deep. In it grows the beginning of a small tree. But a squirrel has captured one of the sunflower seeds and buried it in the pot. A small rain stimulates the seed to grow.*

*The small and crowded pot limits the sunflower seed. But it grows the best it can. It refuses not to grow.*

*Soon, there is a small flower at the top of a rising shoot. It is very small. In fact, the sunflower is scrawny.*

*Still, even if it is scrawny, to me it is beautiful. It is beautiful because it refused not to grow.*

# I PUBLISH,
# YOU PERISH

### For Little Ben

**It is 1987**.

We are now in the present. Only people who are older can personally recall the Great Depression, days of desperation, days of hunger. Model-T cars are funny today, putt-putt-putt. To us, then, they were an awesome back-yard vehicle to the entire county. Yes, I said county. Big stuff. "Tennis" shoes and faded, discolored jeans are back, but they are no longer the clothing of the suffering poor. They are yuppie trendy. (Strange.) People cry at the Vietnam Memorial. Men cry when they arrive there. Men have always cried. Those who tell you they don't are out to bend your brain sideways. The old war continues. It is the same war of 1932, 1945, 1960, 1980, 1550, 1300, and before, long before, (name any year) it is all in a mental jumble of memories and recorded history. It is the war of people, ordinary people, in their struggle to survive, to provide, to care for their children, and to prepare them to fight against the evils that await when they leave home.

*Oh, God, let our child be healthy. Please, let our child be healthy. Let this child grow. Let this child be healthy and grow.*

It is 1987 and many parents are fighting the evils that await their children not after they leave home, but *before.* It is drugs. There is fear in the land. But the fear is not felt by everyone. In a strange world, this is very strange.

One person who has felt the fear is my neighbor, Ted Nelson. So has his wife. They live on the next block. We have been neighbors for some twenty years, and I have followed their family since their youngest son was born. Oh, they were proud of their Little Ben. Tricycle, skateboard, bicycle, vacations, hamster, cat, dog, and all of a sudden it was time for high school.

Ted Nelson and I exchanged rides to work, and during these times we talked of many things. That was when he began to talk to me about Ben. Their kid had become irritable, changing moods from one minute to the next. Then he began to neglect his homework. One thing led to another, and ultimately Ben was expelled from school. The son wanted a car, to get a job he had said. A job was better than nothing, so he got his car. But there was no job, and now Ben was gone from home more often than he had been before the automobile.

Then came the telephone calls at all hours of the day and night, almost always from pay-phones, never last names. The Nelsons fluctuated between believing that Ben had a case of growing pains coupled with ordinary teen-age rebellion, and a frightening conviction that something was seriously wrong. When the family doctor requested a urine test, the Nelsons agreed, certain that the test was more routine than anything specific. Results: cocaine, marijuana.

Not Little Ben. Yes, Little Ben. Experimenting. Surely the boy was only experimenting. Even some professional health workers said that experimenting with drugs was common, and that often it led to nothing serious. "It is a harmless stage," they said. Drugs harmless? His doctor strongly insisted that something should be done immediately. The boy had lost weight. Almost six-feet tall, he was down to a little over 120 pounds.

Ben was not only a good-looking kid, he was also a superb actor. He was able to convince his parents that the doctor's discovery was a one-time experience. "We wanted to believe, so we believed," his father told me. "He couldn't, he couldn't. But he did." There was agony in his face. Later there were tears.

Then there was anger, and hate. But he didn't know who to hate. The telephone calls from people with no last names? "People with no last names, look out for them," he told me. There was a tone of torment in his voice which transcended the ages that we read about in history books. His voice was like that of any worried parent of the 1300's, of the 1500's, of the 1920's, 1960's, now talking to me in 1987.

Then came Ben's thefts of money, stolen credit cards, forged checks. Ben had taken to staying away from home for days at a time.

During one of those absences, his parents tracked him down at a dormitory populated by students of a nearby public university. The dorm was known for its "liberal" life-style, and its inhabitants were largely smart-aleck college students who hated just about everything in the entire world except themselves, even though their dorm was probably the dirtiest place in the entire state of California. I know. Ted Nelson took me to see that students' filthy dorm. All over the walls were murals calling the police pigs. After walking through that dorm, pigs is a very high compliment.

That's the place into which high school teenagers like Ben were invited.

Two deaths of young people from overdoses of heroin at that university students' dorm. Seven taken to a local hospital suffering from LSD overdoses at a "wine party." You don't hear that and then believe that these were isolated incidents. Nor do you believe, as the dorm residents and administrators would have it, when confronted with these tragedies, that over one-hundred and seventy residents in the place saw no evil, heard no evil, did no evil. It all leads you to think that something has been administratively suppressed at this public university students' dormitory. Think of it. Deaths from drug overdoses, hospitalization because of drugs, and no one in the dorm saw, heard, or did anything except to say that the serious drug problems were all caused by alleged outsiders who systematically invaded their dorm for heroin, cocaine, and LSD parties while the residents and administrators innocently slept, or studied, or administered. They call themselves liberals, "an alternative lifestyle," they claimed, but they remind me of the hard-core Nazis who were masters at blaming outsiders for every ill that transpired while trying to convince the world that they were absolutely pure.

That's what my neighbor and I talked about as we struggled with the problem of Little Ben. One day Ted said, *"Everybody wants a quick fix."* Hours later, while I did something at work, his comment came back to me. Then I thought that this is a nation bent on the quick fix. Almost all of television advertising is based on the quick fix. Such simple solutions, just buy the product and your problems will all go away. A car, a deodorant, a candy bar, clothes, a cereal, toothpaste, headache remedies, get any of them and you will be happy beyond your fondest dreams. Television advertising does not sell products, it sells the quick fix. I think that between TV advertising and contemporary American liberalism, the cards are stacked against the present generation of kids. For some time, now, there has been a trend away from social and political liberalism in the nation. And recently, people are tending to move away from watching so much television. I think that the gut-wisdom of the people is at work here. I think that this is a part of the same people's war of the ages, to make the world a better and safer place for their children, to lessen the dangers that await them when they leave home, and to warn them about the dangers that remain.

But what of those for whom it is too late, like Little Ben? Or is it?

On the way to work one day, Ted said, *Little Ben is in rehab. It was that or leave home.* (There were tears in his eyes. For as long as I live, I will never forget that look of haunted agony on his face.) *He took to stealing from us. Credit cards, money, anything he could get his hands on. His mother is really broken up, especially when he tried to forge a couple of checks. I tell you this in a couple of minutes, but I'm talking months, maybe years. A kid stealing from his own parents? And I'm not talking pennies. Then he comes home with a knife cut on his jacket. The calls from people with no last names continued, still from pay phones. That's what they said, the lying bastards. Look, I've read just about everything about drugs lately, but nothing has described the agony, my agony, his mother's agony, Little Ben's agony before the drugs killed off his feeling. Sleepless nights when he was gone. Sleepless nights when he was home. Sometimes I think the main purpose of drugs is to kill parents. But the kids die, too. Look at those who died at that dormitory. The quick fix is really death which comes closer and closer, faster and faster each day, closing in. You see your kid dying, and you are dying, too. And, pretty soon, you can't help but come to hate those young, smart-ass, big-mouth, know-it-all college meat-head kids who still think that drugs are cool, who march against Apartheid, wail for the homeless, and paint murals denouncing injustice while all the time within their walls some are high on cocaine. And if you hate them, do you hate your own kid? Do you hate the bureaucratic bastards who refuse to take a stand while even their own families are in danger? So once again I see the face of death, and once again I've got to fight it. I've got to fight it with everything I've got. Why? He's my kid. He's our kid. He's your kid, and even the kids of the bureaucratic bastards. So you do what you thought you would never do. It is drug rehabilitation or get out of the house.*

*Ben took rehab. We left him there yesterday. Do you know what it is like to tell your own kid you will throw him out of the house? And all the time you know that he is sick and desperately needs help? You threaten to send him out to be with others like him, and that is very frightening. But we have done everything, everything. You can't believe what it has been like. My heart goes out to all those thousands of parents and kids who are facing daily what we are living through. Today I feel even more tired than I have been for as long as I can remember. Your kid becomes a part of every little bit of your life, and every little bit, the color of a wall, a street, a piece of music, the voice of a stranger, a car, everything reminds you of him. It all reminds you of him because you have carried him in your heart and he has been a part of your soul from the very day he was conceived. I'm tired. I don't know what else I can do. Neither does his mother. She is tired, too. Do you know what it is like for a mother to throw her own kid out when all her instincts are screaming against it? I've got to pray. I've got to pray, for him, for us, for strength to go on.*

We met during the lunch hour, and I wondered how he could possibly have gone to work. He had to, I know. But I still wondered. Ted wanted to go to a nearby Catholic church where someone had built a grotto. It was a small structure behind the church, hidden from view by tall bushes. Set in the middle was a statue of a saint. Like most such statues, she was in a prayerful stance, looking very sad. Ted kneeled to pray, and as he did he told me that he had not prayed in over twenty years. I kneeled beside him.

*I come to pray for help. I pray to you for the soul of Little Ben. I pray that you will help his mother. I also pray for the thousands of others who find themselves in the same situation. Please. Just two weeks in rehab, that's all I ask. If he can stay two weeks it will be a good start. Help him do that. If this happens, I promise you a red rose. I promise.*

Ben lasted only six days in the hospital's

drug rehabilitation unit, then he ran away. On the following day he showed up at home. But the deal had been that he complete rehab or leave. He left, but only after getting a few of his things to sell or trade for drugs. He was gone for a month. There was an arrest, then he showed up at home again. His father and mother weakened. They were so glad he was alive they almost forgot about the drugs. "You can stay here, Ben." Perhaps they could talk him into returning for rehabilitation. The son said he would, but for now he was going out for a couple of hours. This time they didn't see him for three weeks. As before, there were no calls, no information. He just disappeared. With knife cuts on his jacket, and an innocent look on his face, he returned on Christmas Day. Ted called me that afternoon.

*He appears to be his old self. But we have been through so much, and we didn't even know if he would be home for Christmas, we didn't buy him anything. We've come to this, not even buying our own son something for Christmas. But you should have seen his face when we told him that he was not getting the traditional family gift of money. It's clear why he came home today.*

Two nights later, Little Ben overdosed in the bathroom. Picture your child dying of drugs in the bathroom of the home for which you worked over twenty years. He almost died. After a night in the hospital, he was taken to a drug rehabilitation program that focuses on both the detox and the psychiatric.  He threatened to leave again, but the staff talked him into signing a contract to remain for at least six weeks.  His parents were also asked to sign the contract. When two weeks passed and Little Ben had not run away, Ted and I returned to the grotto.

*I am keeping my promise.  Little Ben has been in rehab for two weeks.  Here is your red rose.  But you know what?  It took an overdose.  You sure play rough.*

That was all he said, out loud.  He remained kneeling for some time, praying silently.  I don't know if he promised anything more.  I imagine he did, because two weeks is such little time in the rehabilitation process.  I guess Ted thought that if Little Ben could tough it out for two weeks, the odds might begin to turn in his favor.  The rehab process, however, takes a very long, long time.  And sometimes it doesn't work.  If things go well, I think that during the coming months Ted will buy more red roses.

I remember Little Ben when he was beginning to talk.  He used to say "yegalow" for yellow.  And I remember him on his first tricycle.  As he rode it along the sidewalk, he imitated the sound of a motor: "Zummmm. Zummmm."  All of a sudden, it was time for high school.  One day I asked him if drugs were a problem in high school.  "They're into junior high schools," he replied.

I think again of that public university student's dormitory which has become known throughout the area as a center for drug use. Its students and administrators proclaim it to be a major center for an "alternative lifestyle" populated by "liberal" students. Its residents still rail against all the evils in the world. Their hate for the "system" screams out from the dirty murals on their walls. But when youth die of drugs within the confines of their dormitory, and others are carried away to hospitals because, as people say, of countless drug parties, almost two-hundred resident university students suddenly become totally mute: they see no evil, hear no evil, do no evil. Both resident university students and dorm administrators blame "outsiders," and loudly proclaim their own innocence. They have witnessed death and untold suffering all around them, yet they remain silent and do nothing, nothing, nothing, like good and obedient Nazi soldiers.

And finally, after so long, I understand why the gut-American wisdom has turned against this type of "alternative" contemporary liberalism. It is really Neo-Nazism in disguise. It is composed of people who are indifferent to those who die in the drug ovens, especially when those ovens are inside their own building.

Little Ben, this one's for you.

Last night, on television, I saw a person described as a university "expert on drug use." He spent his time talking about his pet theory.

He publishes, Little Ben. You perish.

*It is 1987.*

*And this is for Don José Ruiz, gone now.*

A Light.  A Tree.  A Voyage.  A Tourist.  A Migrant.  A Visitor.

A Light.  A Tree.  A Tourist.  A Migrant.

A Migrant.

A Tourist.   A Migrant on earth..

I. You. We. They. Us.

Today he died.

Don José.

To pluck cotton.  To rest in the heat.  To drink cool, fresh water.  To give a daughter's hand in marriage.  To read, to write, to welcome. To defend a son, to be defended by a son.  To build a house, to build a home.  To make a small house big.  To make a big home small.  To fight prudently.  To laugh prudently.  To speak prudently.  To plant trees.  To lend comfort to the living.  To walk with the dead.

A time to live, and a time to die.  The time of Don José.

# J.F.K.

It is a November evening and the news media is full of accounts about the 25th anniversary of the assassination of President John F. Kennedy.

I am sitting at my computer, checking, rechecking, editing a new manuscript.

Off to the side, at a safe distance from the computer, is the television set. It is turned on, low volume. It drones on and on as I work. It is a habit, like waiting for the daily mail, even though I know that ninety-five percent of it will be junk.

Then the television catches my attention. There is a documentary showing actual clips of the murder of President Kennedy.

I glance and return to work. Moments later, I hear the drum rolls. I look and again I see the funeral procession. Newscasters' voices choke as they narrate the events that unfold before them.

My soul is transported back to another time, another street, another garden, another house and another television set. I am standing before it at midday, my right hand stretched out, leaning against the set as I stare in disbelief, wanting and trying to stop crying long enough to tell my wife that John F. Kennedy is dead.

In less time than it takes to blink, my soul has traveled across time and space, through another dimension, and then returned to this body which has always housed a political cynic. And, even now, so many years later, I choke again.

My reverie is rudely interrupted by one of television's raucous, ear-splitting, crass, greedy, crappy, cruddy, loud commercials that now arrogantly intrudes into history, my history, your history, our history.

Oh, yes, I know *all* the arguments. Life must go on, they say. But is gnawing on bones the definition of life?

At this historic funeral of an American president, I hear it interrupted by television's messages of toilet paper, lingerie, raisins and fast automobiles.

Inside I cry. Outside I laugh.

I turn off the television set and return to my work. In the ensuing silence, I think.

Well, President Kennedy, at least this time television's talking toilets did not interrupt your funeral.

*Count your blessings,* they always say.

But, *don't count your chickens* . . . .

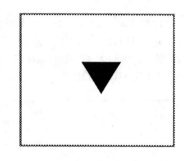

It is 1988, and I am leaving a tall office building, walking toward the parking structure next door.

A woman is walking behind me as I approach two double doors. At the first one, I open the door and hold it for her. She says, "Thank you." I hold the second one open, and she repeats, "Thank you." She passes me and walks ahead.

We walk toward the elevator. She enters it and turns toward the door. She is looking at me. As I approach the elevator, the door closes in my face.

▼

# COMPETITIVE SUFFERING

I like hot dogs and hamburgers, football and tennis. I drive an American-made car, teach my university classes in English, and I've traveled from California to Washington D.C., as well as to Williamsburg, Virginia. I served in the Army of the United States and went to college on the Veterans' G.I. Bill. While I was born in Mexico of Mexican parents, today I consider myself reasonably well-adjusted to life as an American citizen who has flour, corn tortillas, and jalapeños readily available at the local supermarket.

Except.

Except for two things in contemporary American life.

Perhaps I am not as well-adjusted as I thought.

The two things that I have not adjusted to are, (1) the practice of interrupting others when they are speaking, and (2) the ability to engage in competitive suffering. I have never mastered these two forms of modern American discourse. Let me explain.

One day, after work in early 1984, I was watching television and on the screen were several presidential hopefuls debating the issues of the day. Did I say debating? In truth, they were uncouth, constantly interrupting each other, smiling all the while, and trying their best to prevent everyone else from finishing a sentence. Some even succeeded. The audience, in turn, responded as if this were the natural order of the universe, apparently not minding that they might never know what a particular candidate was about to say at a particular moment before he was interrupted by a crescendo of voices around him.

Invariably, following a flurry of uncontrolled interruptions, one of the "debaters" seeking the office of the president would emerge triumphant and trumpet his opinion for all the world to see and hear through the miracle of television.

And that is precisely the process I've never managed to master, the art of continually interrupting until I emerge as the principal speaker. Perhaps it is all because of my early childhood training. Or, perhaps the problem is not cross-cultural but generational. Oh, well, whatever.

I guess I'm doomed.

I guess I'll just continue going to the same neighborhood store, strike up a conversation with the clerk, and never finish because of his interruptions.  And I guess I'll just have to resign myself to failure at faculty meetings because I still signal with my hand when I have something to say, while my colleagues ignore me and go right on interrupting each other.  It all reminds me of a free-speech advocate on campus who would never let me finish a sentence.

It appears that I'll never really adjust to this contemporary American custom even though my students continually interrupt each other during class discussions, faculty do it during meetings, the clerks do it in stores, and everyone does it on radio talk-shows.

Now, don't get me wrong.  I don't mean to say that I never interrupt people when they are speaking.  In fact, in my zeal to fit right in with those around me, I've actually practiced the art of interrupting for years. (As a prime example of downright uncouth interrupting, I've used the McLaughlin Group on educational television.)  Meanwhile, I have listened diligently to someone speak and wait for that certain pause during which I can cut in quickly with my comments.  But I've not been too successful.  First, I spend so much effort waiting for that pause that I fail to grasp what the other person is saying. Maybe what the other person is saying is not that important.  I don't know. And second, after I cut in and speak, invariably the other person says, "Well, it's much more complex than that," thereby politely calling me a simpleton and saying outright that my comments were hardly worth noticing.

Sometimes I think it is the communication professionals who are to blame for all of this because they focus entirely on communicating, meaning how to get your message across. In all my years, I've never heard of an expert in communication who teaches people how to listen.

Perhaps I can become a professional expert in communication. I would specialize in teaching people how to listen. That way, I could talk all I want and no one would interrupt.

Not only have I been unable to master the art of interrupting, I have also failed in the field of competitive suffering.

I began to notice this shortcoming years ago when I went off to college in California and then New Mexico. I recall that when I had a problem or problems, I would tell someone my troubles. But always the listener suffered more. It seemed that everyone around me was more unhappy and undergoing more tribulations than I. Those acquaintances proceeded to inform me that they were having a terrible time not for just one day, but during the entire school year, or the past ten years, or one hundred and more, even up to one-thousand and three-thousand years! Individual people, ethnic groups, racial groups, national groups, and even religious groups all cast themselves into perpetual roles of suffering. And when they did, I felt smaller and smaller.

Before this cosmic condition, I and my problems paled into utter insignificance.

Then I stopped telling anyone my troubles because I did not want to always end up feeling inferior in the face of superior suffering.

That's it, morally inferior. It was a competition to see who suffered the most. And those people who believed they did, ended up with the advantage, perhaps even a morally superior advantage. Those people had suffer power. I didn't.

Years later, when I ran into people I had known in those days, they fondly remembered them as the "good old days." I remembered them as days of competitive suffering. But what can you expect? After all, this is a competitive society.

Suffer power was institutionalized nationally during the Sixties when the War on Poverty officials set up tribunals throughout the land to which people came to compete with each other to see who suffered the most. Those who did, it was believed, would get the most money. It was a form of competitive free-enterprise for the poor. But the poor did not have research centers, departments of social sciences, welfare professionals, and banks of statistical data with which to prove really, really, really big suffering. Presto, enter the surrogate sufferers, young and old professionals who proceeded to compete with each other for monies, each trying to prove that "their people" suffered the most. And presto, again, most of the money went to the professionals and their projects. I guess there is something to this question of competitive suffering, even if it is surrogate suffering. Lots of money in it for the experts.

Sure. I tried to compete, but my grant proposals were always turned down.

The Sixties ended, then the Seventies faded into the past, but competitive suffering went on; past suffering, present suffering, future suffering, it is all around us. Today, unspeakable doom awaits us all if we do not vote for this or that person for president. And when one takes office, then future suffering becomes present suffering because his policies are said to create misery and agony for untold numbers. Meanwhile, teachers in public schools and colleges are also constantly on the edge of doom. My God, can't something be done for them? Why, just the other day, I heard a university president speak against the fiscal Huns who were on the verge of totally destroying his bastion of CIVILIZATION. The valiant and embattled university president said that if he did not prevail against the legislative barbarians, then surely we would enter a new and even darker Dark Age. Now, I ask you, are my stinking little problems more important than that? Clearly, if I ask that question, then I have not mastered the art of competitive suffering.

All around me, husbands, wives, professors, bosses, large families, all are saying they are being subjected to untold suffering. Women, students, nurses, doctors, Blacks, Jews, Chicanos, Asians, Appalachians, the aged, alcoholics, counter-culturalists, not to mention psychiatrists who suffer burnout (a condition believed to be worse than that of any of their patients'), all are competing to see who suffers the most. And I want to help them all. Perhaps in this way I can atone for the social sin of not being a superior sufferer. I feel marginal, alienated, unadjusted. I simply cannot compete against all of that suffering.

Some time ago a friend was telling me his troubles, and his people's troubles, going all the way back to the Paleolithic, it seemed to me. In frustration, I told him that I suffered more than he or any of his group. He got mad. To this day, he will greet me only with an icy distance. How dare I attempt to take away his most precious competitive weapon?

I guess when all is said and done, my failure in the art of interrupting, and my inability to join in competitive suffering are just examples of my being culturally disadvantaged, or a slow learner, or a person with a cognitive dysfunction, or unacculturated, or with only the right side of my brain working, or my behavior is genetically determined, or all of the above and more.

Now, if this is true, a whole lot of professional experts are going to make a lot of money off of my handicaps. They're going to pick my bones dry.

But I am growing old. Can you imagine an older person who is culturally disadvantaged, a slow learner, with a cognitive dysfunction, unacculturated, with only half a brain working, and with genetic problems? Wow! That could make some young professional turkeys a lot of money.

I wonder if I will ever see any of it.

Chances are I won't.

Who cares about older people, anyway?

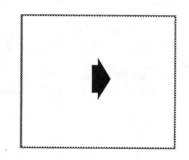

It is 1988, and our son, Chico, walks in the door. He tells us about what happened at an automatic teller machine outside a bank.

He was waiting in line with some other people when a Berkeley panhandler walks up to the man in front of him.

"Excuse me, sir." the panhandler asks politely, "Do you have a quarter?"

"No," the man replies in an unfriendly voice.

"That's too bad," the panhandler says. "I do."

# FUTURE SCHLOCK

It is often said that "Those who are ignorant of their history are doomed to repeat it." To this I would like to add that many people who know their history are also doomed to repeat it, in fact, do so gladly. With this in mind, and with some knowledge of history, I would like to make the following predictions of the future.

## Prediction #1

In the near future, an extensive national survey will be conducted, with random sampling and all. The survey will reveal that more and more Americans of all ages are becoming hard of hearing. Follow-up research will show the prime cause to be the extremely loud television commercials.

To compensate for this spreading affliction, the advertising and television industries will get together and make their television commercials even louder.

## Prediction #2

On a Wednesday morning in 1994, a sports announcer will be found unable to stop talking, though the football game he had been broadcasting had ended three days before. His case becomes well-known, and soon a scientific controversy breaks out. Sociologists will claim that the man's behavior is the result of the social environment. Psychologists will counter with the assertion that it is the result of behavioral conditioning. Anthropologists will insist the root cause is culture, while numerous biologists will call the behavior an obvious case of a predisposing genetic condition.

On his own, the sports announcer will stop talking. However, the scientific controversy will continue for several years.

## Prediction #3

Following the 1980's practice of releasing copies to the media of speeches delivered by the president with inserted comments indicating audience response in parentheses, such as (laughter), (applause), and the like, I predict that a future president, when there is no live audience, will achieve the same end by using a sound track.

## Prediction #4

Universities will continue to graduate psychiatrists until there is a glut in the market, with one psychiatrist for every fifty people. As a consequence, the emerging field of dog psychiatry will grow until there is one for every hundred dogs (one for every twenty dogs in the more affluent neighborhoods). After that, a new specialization will be established: pet fish psychiatry. The new specialty will be dedicated to (1) the proposition that pet fish need help to adjust to the confinement of a fish tank, and (2) the proposition that all psychiatrists need work, or vice-versa.

## Prediction #5

In the near future, what once had been thought totally impossible will be achieved. Television programs will become even worse. When interviewed about this state of affairs, an unnamed television executive will say, "It was necessary. The more horrendous, violent, tragic or meaningless the TV programs are, the greater will be the appeal of the salvation offered by the products advertised on our commercials. That's where the bucks are."

## Prediction #6

Television news readers, incorrectly called news broadcasters today, will be replaced by computerized screen robots. Few people will notice the change.

## Prediction #7

Sometime during the 1990's, a young Black newscaster, having heard news reports all of his life which used the phrase "Black on Black crime," will begin to say, when appropriate, which is quite often, "White on White crime." He will refine the concept to include "Irish on Irish crime," "English on English crime," and the like. Just before he begins to use phrases such as "Irish on Italian crime," or "Jewish on Anglo crime," he will be fired.

## Prediction #8

I predict that sometime in the not too distant future, a very famous, wealthy, aging movie and television star, and his wife of 58 years, will be sued by their adult yuppie son whom they raised in a loving, caring, family oriented home, providing him with the best possible education.

The lawsuit will charge that because he was raised in a loving and nurturing home, his parents therefore deprived him of the opportunity to write a book exposing them. Thus, he will claim, they caused him to lose royalties and substantial advances for movie rights to the story.

The yuppie son and his lawyer will ask for $6,000,000. (The $6,000,000 figure may not be accurate. It is possible plaintiff will ask for $10,000,000 or $15,000,000.)

## Prediction #9

During the mid-1990's, an empathetic bartender will give some friendly advice to a despondent customer whom he has known for several years. Later, the bartender will be arrested, jailed, and charged with practicing psychiatry without a license.

## Prediction #10

Also in the mid-1990's a new record will be set for the showing of movies and TV programs about Nazis, averaging about 25 per day.

## Prediction #11

In the late months of 1992, a west coast city's association of the elderly will hold its annual meeting. The invited speaker will be billed as an expert on the problems of the elderly. He is a young Ph.D. with a doctorate in gerontology from a highly prestigious university.

In the audience will be Mrs. J. Jamison, whose favorite grandson recently committed suicide. Seated next to her will be Jane Childress, a victim of arthritis and recipient of a heart transplant. Behind them is Patricia Maglin who has been mugged four times while on her way to the corner store. A close friend of hers has had her apartment ransacked twice in the past six months. Mr.

Janowski is present. He has bandages on his face and an arm in a sling. His wife is still in the hospital. They were viciously beaten by a burglar at three in the morning. Another elderly person in the audience will exhibit highly nervous behavior. He's a victim of over-prescribed drugs. Virtually all the others in the audience have a similar story to tell, including Marge Gibbert, whose yuppie son is on heroin and visits only to steal from her.

The speaker, in his capacity as an expert on gerontology, will advise the people in the audience to live a healthy life style, to participate in healthful activities, and to avoid stress.

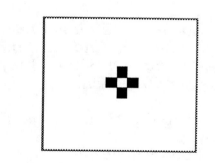

*It is 1988.*

*I am sixty-four years old, going on sixty-five.*

*I am at home in Oakland, California.*

*Across the street, bulby pink nubs grow from the ends of magnolia tree branches.  I see them when  I go there to walk the dogs.*

*Some of the nubs are turning brown.  They are opening and dropping orange and red seeds which shine brightly on the green grass of the lawn.*

*They do this every year.*

*Soon it will be Spring.*

*It is the miracle again.*

✜

# FIVE PAGES

# FOR DAN

Dan died.

I heard about it from a Dominican priest.

"Dan is dead," he said.

The priest had the face of a young boy. There was a look of anger in his eyes, an anger at death, a mirror of the original force that probably propelled him toward the priesthood.

Dan died.

I heard about it from a Dominican priest.

"Dan is dead," he said.

We spoke briefly about it, near the entrance to the church, under a stand of dormant poplar trees. 1989's January was ending. The young priest felt deeply about Dan's death. And, when he told me, I felt a profound sadness, a shock at first, and then a sadness which I could not explain, not to the young priest, not to anyone, not to myself.

Dan died.

I heard about it from a Dominican priest.

"Dan is dead," he said.

I called my two dogs and headed home.

We walked alongside the strong trunks of poplar trees, through a wrought-iron gate, and onto the sidewalk. I looked at the homes across the street. To the left was a two-story duplex, neat, well-painted, with new black asphalt in the driveway. Large "picture" windows adorned the exterior of the building. As my gaze moved along the neighboring homes, I looked at a stately Victorian house with a full-grown magnolia tree in the center of the large front yard. Then I looked at the superbly neat, white-painted home next to the Victorian. The homes along this street are solidly middle-class. Inside them there is warmth, shelter, food.

"Dan is dead," he said. The houses were silent. Walls, bricks, fireplaces, floors and windows do not speak of living and dying. Only people can do that. And, although we live scant yards from each other, we do not speak of living and dying, not to each other, though we are neighbors. "Dan is dead," he said. The young Dominican priest was right. Dan was/is dead.

Dan was a bum. He was a bum to some people. To others, he was just plain no good, a tramp. Dan was a wino. He was alcoholic. And he was young. Oh, so young. Some people pegged him to be in his early thirties. I pegged him in his mid-twenties. Either way, he looked old, especially when he walked, slow, tired, drunk. I remember the

first time I saw him up close, and my surprise at his youth.

One day, Dan appeared in our neighborhood, where he became a walker of the
streets, an unsteady walker, a shuffler, a sitter under trees, a sitter on sidewalks, a
sleeper on cement and on the ground, under
the spreading branches of a pine tree, and
hidden from street-view by a clump of bushes, including a rose bush which gave pink
blossoms but I don't remember if it did
while Dan was sleeping there.

Dan had a dog, a police-spaniel-cocker
dog of dried blood color, a dog that walked
with him, shuffled with him, sat and slept
with him, looked at him, lived with him.
Every day, and every night, the dog was with
him.

Once in days past, Dan's hair must have
been shorter and a golden blond. Now it was
fairly long and knotted from a lack of comb-
ing, brownish from a lack of washing.

In my mind I have a picture of Dan, about
five-foot-ten, lanky, a freckled round face,
and dressed in tan-colored clothes, always
wearing tan, unlaundered, of course. His dog
looked unlaundered, but never hungry.

One day I heard that the police had
picked up Dan who ended up in de-tox at a
local hospital. His dog was taken to the dog
pound where, everybody knew, unclaimed
dogs were not kept long, and paid-for-
vaccinations were necessary before release.

Dan didn't have money for dog vaccinations. I knew that. Then, for several days, I
saw Dan walking around alone, and I won-

dered whether or not to broach the subject of his dog. Look! There! under those trees! There he is, with his dog beside him!

"I went and got him at the dog pound," he told me in such a matter-of-fact voice that I felt dumb. The pound was at least eight miles away, across freeways, dozens of intersections, and through strange neighborhoods. Yet, there they were, shuffling, moving from one place to another, like nothing at all had happened.

They shuffled off together and sat under a maple tree. Dan took out a plastic container, such as those dispensed at a fast food restaurant, and gave the contents to his dog. The dog ate as Dan drank from his bottle.

There was a time, not too long ago, when Dan took to sleeping behind some bushes in the seminary grounds across the street from our house. On occasion, at night, I would hear him scream loudly at the devils who were hounding him, and hounding him. I imagine other neighbors heard Dan, and I'm sure there was some muttering. Screams in the night make some people nervous. Other people became nervous because children walked by there mornings and afternoons on their way to, and from, a grammar school up the street. It was about that time, unfortunately, when Dan took to urinating in the open, in the daylight, next to a small hedge, near to where the children walked by. Some people became very upset over this. I don't know if they called the police or not, but shortly after that Dan disappeared again. I say again, because this happened regularly.

"No trespassing. Private Property" said the sign at the entrance gate to the seminary grounds. Poor Dan. Did he know he had tread on God's private property? Did he know he'd peed on it?

Nevertheless, some of the sons and daughters of Dominic and of Thomas Aquinas cared for Dan. I mean cared in both senses of the word. They took care of him as best they could, did what they could, and they accepted him as a human being. By that I mean, they talked to him. They spoke gently. And by that I mean, they stood close to him and looked him gently in the eye. Which is something virtually no one else would do with Dan. People were never close to him. In my mind, I see Dan again. And in this mental image I see Dan sitting on the sidewalk on the avenue, where restaurants and specialty stores abound. I see yuppies rush by with little bags of marinated olives and salmon mousse in their hands. They walk by Dan and his dog. And there is that distance between them, and isn't this the way it is and always will be?

There was always that distance between Dan and other people, between Dan and the neighbors, between Dan and me, between my dogs and his dog. One time, one of my dogs tried to make friends with his dog. As they sniffed each other, their tails wagged while their bodies were stiff and alert. Dan called his dog back. I did the same. After that, our dogs stayed away from each other.

Distance. A bubble of distance surrounded Dan and his dog wherever they went. Physical distance. Social distance, Psychological distance and anthropological distance. Economic distance.

But let me tell you, Dan was a hard worker, a very hard worker. He probably put in more hours each day than most working people, driven as he was by an imperative that demanded every ounce of his waning energy, every day, and into every night. In his condition, to move from one corner of a city block to the next must have been like walking three blocks, maybe more, as he and his dog tread slowly along, noticed but not seen.

One sunny day, he tried to tell me about his father, but his words, although he tried hard, were a disjointed jumble of sounds. All I remember of this brief instant is that Dan tried to tell me about his father.

Dan begged for alms.

The Dominicans began as a mendicant order.

Now, in my mind, I see a young Dominican priest, standing face to face with Dan. And I ask in that silent way of the imagination, who is the priest and who is the beggar? Strange question? It arises from the depths of my past, from childhood when I heard the adults speak. I learned the way children learn, by synthesis, without listening, by seeming always to be someplace else, by human radar, by tone of voice. It was then I learned that equals do not need each other, but unequals do. I learned that by synthesis, without listening, and it returns now as my mind reconstructs the vision of Dan and the

Dominican, standing face to face, as voices from the past buzz in my mind, voices of people now dead, like Dan.

"Dan is dead," said the Dominican priest who had known him probably better than anyone else. Services for his body and soul were held at a local Methodist church. Attending were four Dominican nuns and several priests. "I was surprised at how many people were there," added the young priest, "I guess some of them were people who had got to know him along the avenue."

I had not known about Dan's death. When he said that he and his Dominican colleagues had attended the services, and other people had been there also, I felt a tinge of relief. Still, the sadness remained. Later the same day, I wanted to write something about Dan, but for several days nothing but blank pages came to mind, over and over. A week went by and still blank pages occupied my mind. When nothing came to me, I decided on a different approach. I would pick a number of pages, and go from there. One or two pages, I thought, would not mean anything. And three pages would be only a token. Then I thought of five pages. At least that would show some respect. In a flash, the very second this came to me, I thought of the title: *Five Pages For Dan.* Yes, that was it. But now I had a title and still the rest remained blank. It remained like this for several days.

Finally, I felt it would not be proper to let any more time pass. I took out five blank pages, and printed the title on the first. "I will fill them," I said to myself. "For Dan."

**+**

Dan died.
I heard about it from a Dominican priest.
"Dan is dead," he said.

**+**

Dan died.
I heard about it from a Dominican priest.
"Dan is dead," he said.

**+**

Dan died.
I heard about it from a Dominican priest.
"Dan is dead," he said.

And when he told me, I felt a deep sadness, a shock at first, and then a sadness which I could not explain, not to the young priest, not to anyone, not to myself.

Hey, God, can you hear me?

Listen, God. Since Dan died, three others have taken his place. Can you hear me?

God?

*It is 1988.*

*I am hungry for a snack. Walking down the street, I stop to purchase a bag of tortilla chips. From habit, I turn the bag to read the ingredients. What hath God wrought?*

**Ingredients:** Corn, Vegetable Oil (Contains one or more of the following: Corn Oil, Sunflower Oil, Cottonseed Oil, Partially Hydrogenated Sunflower Oil, Partially Hydrogenated Soybean Oil, and/or Peanut Oil), Buttermilk, Salt, Tomato, Partially Hydrogenated Soybean Oil, Corn Syrup Solids, Whey, Onion, Imitation Parsley (Starch, Gum Arabic, Gelatin, Glycerol, and Artificial Colors), Garlic, Monosodium Glutamate, Cheddar Cheese (Milk, Cheese Culture, Salt, Calcium Chloride, and Enzymes), Sugar, Nonfat Milk, Dextrose, Soy Grits, Malic Acid, Sodium Caseinate, Natural and Artificial Flavors, Sodium Acetate, Mono & Diglycerides, Dipotassium Phosphate, Spice, Citric Acid, Sodium Citrate, Disodium Inosinate, Disodium Guanylate, and Artificial Colors (Including Yellow #5).

*This is not like grandmother used to make, or even mother. Neither one of them went to college and learned all about chemicals and stuff.*

*I guess they were just "uneducated."*

**66**

# FIRST LINE

Below is an opening line for a novel, and how I believe some university professors would write the same thought.

*"When Leonard woke up that morning, his first impulse was to get even with Max, although his mother, who was still asleep in the next room, had told him to forget it, let it be."*

### Sociologist

When Leonard woke up that morning in his lower middle-class home, he felt the social system had failed him, leaving him with his mother, an upwardly mobile single parent as his only significant other.

## Anthropologist

Leonard woke up. Waking up was a custom of his culture, handed down from generation to generation. In the next room was the person he called 'mother' (muh-thr), a linguistic term handed down from generation to generation. Leonard wanted to get even with Max. His cultural values, as handed down from generation to generation, required that he do so. His mother (muh-thr) was against it, just as mothers (muh-thrs) had done from generation to generation in his culture. Before Leonard went downstairs, he went to pee. He peed downward instead of up. This custom had been handed down in his culture from generation to generation.

## Psychologist

When Leonard woke up that morning, he wanted to get even with Max, but first he had to deal with an intervening variable, his mother. A research plan slowly formed in his mind.

## Psychiatrist

When Leonard woke up, it was clear he was in need of professional counseling in order to understand his feelings. His mother, in the next room, also needed counseling in order to resolve the conflict with her son. Her employer would also need counseling in order to learn to deal with employees who needed counseling.

## Engineer

Leonard was nuts. He had a screw loose somewhere. You could tell when he bolted upright in bed so quick that he wrenched his back. In the next room, his mother was looking for her bridge. Nothing a good engineer couldn't fix.

## Nutritionist

When Leonard woke up that morning, his first impulse was to get even with Max, but only after a breakfast of soft-boiled eggs, whole wheat toast with low cholesterol margarine, orange juice, and a glass of low-fat milk. Once, in a fit of teenage rebellion, he substituted tomato juice for the orange.

## Epidemiologist

When Leonard woke up that morning, his first impulse was to get even with Max for breathing in his face, giving him the flu. He didn't need a psychologist, or a psychiatrist, or a sociologist. He didn't need any of those pseudo scientists. All he needed was the consummate skill of one damn good epidemiologist, and there's plenty of those around.

## Surgeon

When Leonard woke up that morning, his first impulse was to cut right down to the heart of the matter.

## Football Coach

Lenard had the fiting spirut.  When he awoked up, he decided to tackel the situation with Max, even thou he new that Max was on gard  His gameplan was to have his mama remain in the sidelines, and be a man for once.

## Ethnic Studies

When Leonard woke up that morning, he felt alone, abandoned, that the world was against him.  "This must be how ethnic minorities must feel," he thought to himself.

## Biologist

When Leonard woke up, his first impulse was to get even with Max.  Was this hereditary?  After all, just the day before, his mother had said, "You're just like your father!"

## Forestry

When Leonard woke up, he looked at the panels of ash on the walls, then at the oak floor.  His first impulse was to get even with Max, who lived in a redwood house.

## Computer Sciences

When Leonard woke up, he had an internal drive to get even with Max.  In the next room, his mother worried about paying for the utilities, and that her son would not be able to suppress his surge of anger.

## Health Educator

When Leonard woke up, his first impulse was to get even with Max, then stop smoking.  He had no time to think of the dental checkup scheduled for 10:15 that morning. In the next room, his mother wondered if he had brushed his teeth before going to bed. "He should cut down on sugar," she thought.

## Religious Studies

When Leonard woke up that morning, he had already decided to raise Cain with Max. "An eye for an eye," he thought.  "None of that turn the other cheek stuff for me."

## Journalism

It was the morning that a three-alarm fire killed two people in an apartment building, not far from the freeway accident that left four people dead. Almost at the same time, an airplane crash in the next county killed fifteen passengers, spilling diesel fuel into a stream, killing many fish. It was almost at the same time that a train in Britain derailed that Leonard woke up. He did not know that the train accident killed six commuters, while ethnic riots in Russia left fifteen people dead. Leonard looked at the large oak tree across the street. It was similar to the oak tree under which the victims of a mass murder had been found just four days before.

A police car, responding to the call to investigate, was struck by a big-rig, killing the officer. The truck overturned, falling atop a cat that had been by the side of the road. The cat died instantly.


### Economist

Leonard woke up. On the other hand, it may have been Max. His first impulse, all things being equal, was to balance accounts with Max. On his dresser lay a glove for the left hand. On the other hand, it may have been worn on the other hand.

*It is 1988, and I really don't ever expect to find myself meditating high atop an isolated and fog-enshrouded mountain.*

*Nor do I ever expect that, if I did, another human being would climb that mountain in order to ask me a question.*

*But, if all this came to pass, no matter what the question, I would answer:*

"Go forth and tell the people.

Yesterday is the past,
and, yesteryear is the present.

Tell no one under thirty.

They wouldn't understand."

# TO HATE - WITH LOVE

Over the years, many times, I have heard people say the same words, in California, New Mexico, Texas, in the army, in college, from neighbors, companions, friends and peers, in a cotton field in Texas, in a pup tent in Normandy, from a master weaver of rugs in New Mexico, and from an auto mechanic in Yuma, Arizona.

The sounds of their voices come back to me, words in passing, words exchanged during a party with close friends, words at work, words in a noisy bar, and words whispered in the night.

"I hated it!" Those were the words.

They came back to me yesterday, while breaking rock-hard clumps of clay in the back yard. Then, in my mind, I saw myself as a young kid wielding a heavy pick almost too large for a twelve-year-old, breaking clods, digging a hole, wanting to be done so I could run off and do something else, mainly nothing, hating the task at hand, and slowing down so much that if someone were to look at me they would see a kid doing, well, mainly nothing.

I hated it.

Now, I stood there in my back yard, with pick in hand, perspiring under the mid-summer sun, brown trousers covered with fine dust, and more hard clods to break up so I could prepare the ground for planting, just as I had done when I had been twelve years old, and hated it. As I thought about it, I smiled, with love. "To hate, with love," I said to myself as I lifted the pick once more.

I had finished digging the hole, back then, filled a bucket with water and watched it slowly soak into the soil. Then there was a geranium planted there, and I had helped.

It had been the time of The Great Depression, when people lost a lot. We didn't lose anything because we had nothing. No. I take that back. We had a geranium.

Do you know that in this very day and age, when so much has been accomplished, there are actually thousands of young people who have never once lifted a pick and driven it into the ground?

"To hate, with love." That's what so many people had told me over the years. "I hated it!" they had said as we exchanged smiles of affection for people and things gone by, for memories of when we were young, too young to understand that if someone were to say to us, "To hate, with love," someday it would make perfect sense.

*It is March, 1988.*

*Years ago, at the far corner of the semi-
nary across the street, someone laid out an
outdoor spot for meditation. By a large ponderosa pine, by lush bamboo, with ferns all
about, and a crab apple tree on the side, neat
rectangle slabs of pebbled concrete had been
laid. A large, basaltic boulder was set in the
ground, facing the meditation corner.*

*The boulder has taken on a special mean-
ing for me, a constant in a changing world.
On occasion, when sitting there, I lose myself so that I don't even hear the rush of the
freeway traffic, or the screaming sadness of
sirens in the distance.*

*With a new and noisy freeway nearby, the
spot became a poor place for the novitiates
to meditate. I adopted it, cleaning out the
pine needles and dried grass until it looked
almost new. I often go there and sit quietly
on the boulder.*

*To me, it is an important corner of peace.
Someone worked very hard to place the
boulder there. When I arrive, the first thing I
do is look at it. It makes me feel good. Funny how you can become attached to an inani-
mate object, but that is what happened.*

*Yesterday I went to my special meditation
spot. I had personal worries. I had to think.
I took the dog with me, a good companion
for troubled times. There was the boulder.*

*As I was about to sit down, the dog peed
on it.*

*It is 1988, and I am angry.*

*I am about to retire, and living in a city is the pits. You have no control over anything. You are a victim of everything that happens around you. The only response left is anger.*

*And that is why I was angry about the constant parking of cars in front of our house. Over and over, I arrive home and cannot park in front of our own home. Strangers, all strangers, park and park and park, so I have no place left.*

*On this day, yes, still another car has parked in front of our home, and the months and months of anger accumulated in me until I took our second car and parked it flush against that stranger's automobile, making it impossible for the intruder to leave.*

*That afternoon, I am watering the lawn when a pretty Pilipino girl walks up and gets into the offending car. She has trouble moving her blocked-in car, thanks to me. Heh, heh, heh.*

*All of a sudden, I hear a voice speaking. "Let me help you," the voice says.*

*The next thing I know, I am moving the car I had parked angrily to block her in.*

*I sure hope feminists don't hear about this. They'd try to embarrass me in front of the entire nation, probably they would call me a chauvinist pig.*

It is 1988 and I have bought a new pair of shoes.

When I was young, I could wear any pair of shoes. But now, at my age, I have to get very good shoes with good support or I get tired quickly when I walk around.

I wore the new shoes for a couple of days, and they were indeed good except that on the third day they began to squeak loudly. The more I walked around the house the louder they squeaked.

Squeak...squeak...squeak.

I went into the kitchen and told Olga, "Listen!" as I walked across the room.

She said, "I can't hear anything because your shoes are squeaking too loud."

It is 1988, and I go to the post office in Berkeley. I park across the street, near a bank and a cheese shop.

In front of the bank, by a bed of orange flowers, sit two panhandlers. They are about as dirty as can be, unshaven, and wearing torn clothes. One is bare-foot, the other is wearing leather sandals but no socks. Both have rough, uncut and unwashed long hair. Each one has a sixteen-ounce can of beer from which they drink as the mood suits them.

As I am returning to my car, one of the panhandlers gets up and, with beer can in one hand, he stretches out the other and puts the touch on a man walking ahead of me. The man stops, digs in his pocket, and gives the panhandler some money. While he is waiting for the money, the panhandler takes another drink of beer.

As I walk by, the two panhandlers are joking and laughing.

I return to my car and watch. The same scenario is repeated five times. Three of those are successful. Three of five is pretty good odds.

Well, if my social security is insufficient, I can always go out into the streets of Berkeley, with a beer can in my hand.

*It is June 15, 1988.*

*It is a grumpy day. I am grumpy.*

*All day, I see no good, do no good, and hear no good.*

*In the evening, I see a documentary segment on television. It is about peregrine falcons and how, during the Sixties, they almost became extinct because of pesticides.*

*Then the program turns to a husband and wife, in the Midwest, who have taken it upon themselves to help restore the peregrine population. Carefully, they hatch the eggs in an incubator. They raise the birds and set them free. They do it because they want to.*

*In my mind, I picture the falcons, flying.*

> *Peregrine*
> *Peregrine*
> *Peregrine*

*The name reminds me of a mantra.*

Well, here it is, 1989. A new year begins. I will retire in a few months. And I remember the 1930's.

I think of a fig tree growing in our back yard. As I walk toward the tree, I walk on the earth. There is nothing between me and the earth because I am barefoot. When I am barefoot, the earth and I are one. I walk on the earth and the memory of it is fine, thank you, just fine.

Each year I walk on the earth and I eat figs from the tree.

Some ripen and fall on the ground. I am pretty good at spotting the ripest and sweetest. They are darkest color and their skin is cracking open. They are the hardest to peel. In those days of my childhood, I could scan the tree and immediately tell if there was something sweet to eat there. Often, some of the ripest figs had been partly eaten by the birds, usually the ripest and sweetest.

We knew the same thing, the birds and I. And, because we did, we were kin.

Sometimes I would pluck a partly eaten fig, peel what I could, and eat it. Often I would eat around what the bird had eaten. Other times I would eat it all.

We shared the figs, the birds and I.

I remember.

This year I will plant a fig tree. And I will invite all the birds.

*To be continued.....*